Green
Silence

Books by Ivan T. Sanderson

Animal Treasure
Animals Nobody Knows
Caribbean Treasure
Living Treasure
Animal Tales
How to Know the North American Mammals
The Silver Mink
John and Juan in the Jungle
Living Mammals of the World
Follow the Whale
The Monkey Kingdom

Abominable Snowmen: Legend Come to Life
The Continent We Live On
The Dynasty of Abu
Ivan Sanderson's Book of Great Jungles
This Treasured Land
Uninvited Visitors
"Things"
More "Things"
Invisible Residents
Investigating the Unexplained

As Terence A. Roberts

Mystery Schooner

The Status Quo

Green Silence

Travels Through the Jungles of the Orient

by

Ivan T. Sanderson
F.L.S., F.Z.S., F.R.G.S., M.A. (Cantab.)

Edited by

Sabina W. Sanderson

David McKay Company, Inc.
New York

Green Silence

Frontispiece: Ivan T. Sanderson at Eton, age 16.

LIBRARY OF CONGRESS CATALOG CARD NUMBER: 74–81710
ISBN 0–679–50487–7
MANUFACTURED IN THE UNITED STATES OF AMERICA
DESIGNED BY JACQUES CHAZAUD

Preface

Ivan Sanderson's life was rich enough in incident, adventure, and experience to fill the lives of three ordinary men. This book, which is really the story of the making of a naturalist, covers only a few years of his career, but years that form a sort of *Anlage* period, a time of sowing that was to yield imaginative and intellectual fruit throughout the remainder of his work in many fields of enquiry. He was fortunate enough to fall in love with the natural world early in life and even more fortunate in remaining true to that love for all his days.

He was a wonderful companion. His conversation and company were prized by everyone who knew him well. His makeup had a great deal of the ability to *see,* to pay real attention, that is the first quality required of a naturalist. He also had in him more than a little of the taste for adventure that one finds in Hawkins and Drake.

This book is a testimony to his love for the "earthly paradise," albeit with a raised eyebrow when required and the ability to derive joy and laughter from the contradictory behavior of both men and animals. It is fortunate for us all that he was able to make a rough draft of this book before he died and that his wife, Sabina, was able to complete it and see the book through to the press in line with his intentions. It captures the voice and spirit of a remarkable man. For those who knew Ivan and loved him this is his finest legacy.

JAMES O'SHEA WADE
New York
1974

Contents

Contents

The drawings are by Ivan T. Sanderson, though not all are signed (he sometimes failed to do this because "there's no place to sign it without ruining the design"—which is true). Some of these drawings have been published before but others are "new."

The plans of estates and such were traced from his diary, the only change made being the cross-hatching which I did with a ruler rather than roughly and free-hand. The labels have of course been set in type, but duplicate those written by him.

The maps I did, with a few finishing touches taught me by Ivan.

S. W. S.

The illustrations follow page 106.

Introduction

G*reen Silence* IS THE BOOK
Ivan always wanted to write and one for which he had no
trouble in finding a title, often a most difficult task. He
was originally committed for a quite different kind of
book but lost interest in it and was overjoyed when a
friend published a paperback book on the same subject,
thus giving him a splendid excuse not to do it. His editor
at David McKay Company was delighted to accept *Green
Silence* as a substitute.

Ivan completed only two chapters before his shoulder,
most affected by the cancer that finally took his life, became so painful that he could not type. He then tried
writing in longhand, but even this proved too much, and
he could do only a page or two a day. His handwriting
was not good at the best of times; one of the tutors at

Eton described it as "irritating," and Ivan once told me that my "worst mistake" ever was in admitting that I could read it. He also had the problem that he could think much faster than he could write, which resulted in considerable frustration. We resorted finally to a tape recorder, which was set up in a back room where Ivan could sit comfortably with a drink and cigarettes at hand and record his thoughts without interruption. We also talked for long hours, and I kept paper and pencil at hand, being frequently admonished to "write this down." Some of these notes were specifically to do with *Green Silence,* others were general biographical notes and reminders. And he worked out a general plan for *Green Silence,* one that bore no resemblance to his original typed outline, which was to include tales of all the jungles he had visited. He had, of course, told of some of these in his three "Treasure books"—*Animal Treasure, Living Treasure,* and *Caribbean Treasure*—and he soon concluded that he had more than enough for a book on the jungles of the Oriental region alone.

Ivan died before he could do more, and it was months before I could bring myself to listen to the tape. I then listened to just enough to be certain that I could transcribe it (from a purely technical standpoint), ran it back, and typed the whole thing in one go. Some is very personal, and it is clear that he sensed that he would not live to finish the book. In his cheerier moods he said, "Sabina, we must check this . . ."; at other times his phrase is, "Sabina, you must check on this. . . ." There are many "instructions" on the tape, and it is not a continuous narrative; much of it is of the "No, go back a bit; before I did that I . . ." variety.

My first step, then, was to edit the material on the tape. At first it looked like a great deal, but when I had eliminated some material that was in fact totally foreign to the general theme of the book (but will, I hope, be published later), and extracted the instructions, the directly usable material had shrunk considerably. It was, nevertheless, quite enough to encourage me to inform the publisher that we would have a book after all.

Ivan kept a diary through much of his stay in Indonesia, but not all. It stops abruptly and permanently during one period of illness, and there are other gaps covered only by the briefest of notes, obviously intended as an *aide-mémoire* to be used when he had time to write up his diary properly. Some of these are helpful in that they contain key words, either understandable in themselves or that clearly tie in with one of the notes I took down; others are utterly routine, and a few just plain meaningless to anyone but their author.

The diary nevertheless contained a great deal that I was able to use with only the most minor editorial changes and additions, though in some cases I did indulge in some literary license in that, for example, I combined visits to several plantations in a specific area. I also ignored such things as Ivan's chronic battles with post offices, banks, shipping clerks, and the like. They were naturally important to him at the time but are hardly of interest to anyone else. Long periods when nothing much happened are also omitted for obvious reasons, though this does produce an erroneous picture of a nearly uninterrupted series of "adventures."

Apart from the diary, there were also some letters to his mother, though for the most part these duplicate the diary; and there were several pieces written for publication but, with one exception, never sold. These were perfect for *Green Silence* and were included almost unchanged. Passages from others of his books were sometimes paraphrased, sometimes "lifted" intact, depending on their nature and use. One particularly beautiful paragraph was taken from a science-fiction novel he never finished—it took place in a jungle, of course.

Those episodes in the book for which I had only notes I have told as nearly in Ivan's words as I could, though if there are differences in style, some are the result of the period of forty years that elapsed between the writing of the diary entries and the manuscript started by Ivan specifically for *Green Silence.*

A few "technical" notes may be in order. Ivan was hopeless at names, and many an entry reads "talked with [blank]" or "passed through the village of [blank]," and his spelling was wildly erratic. Place names in Indonesia are subject to considerable variation in spelling anyway, if the names have not been changed altogether in the past forty years. I have used *a* standard spelling for these, but do not guarantee that these are the current standards. In some cases Ivan's spelling of a name would have astonished the Indonesians, but I was usually able to identify the town by measuring on a map the approximate route given in the diary and then indulging in a process of elimination. Some place names cannot be identified, particularly when they refer to estates that are only roughly located as so many miles southwest of such and such a town. Nor can some of his treks into the jungle be pinned down with any exactitude. In one or two instances I have retained the old name in the text but have indicated the modern name in brackets.

I have almost never used personal names, in part because of the occasional "telescoping" of events, in part because I do not know whether they would wish to have their names used, and tracking them down to ask permission is a practical impossibility even if they are still alive.

Scientific names of animals have been included where they could be determined. If simply in some doubt, I have added a question mark, but if the identification is really indeterminate, I have not indicated any name. Information on animals has been gleaned from some of Ivan's other books and, where necessary or desirable, from other standard reference works. I have tried not to turn this into a textbook but at the same time felt it most unfair not to give some description of an animal and its habits, since most of those mentioned will be unknown to most readers. It is hardly necessary to describe a tiger, but a cuscus is not likely to be familiar to many.

In this day and age of "equality for everyone," some of the practices reported or implied in this book may come in for criticism from some readers. I must point out that in 1928 they were universally accepted and unquestioned. Ivan considered Achi his friend, but Achi was also his servant. One did not share a room, dine, or travel in the same class with one's servant; it was not done. And Achi himself would have been horrified (or contemptuous) had Ivan failed to follow the established customs. Privately, they could be, to some extent, two boys adventuring on their own; publicly, form had to be strictly adhered to. According to Ivan, Achi carried out all the duties of a servant, even when they were "hopelessly lost" in Celebes, refusing to allow Ivan to so much as carry water or light a fire; that was Achi's job. Even when there were urgent and practical reasons for "bending the rules," Achi did so only under protest. On the other hand, like all superb servants, he was a master of the tactfully offered suggestion (usually translatable as "no, you blithering idiot, don't do it that way"), and Ivan learned much from him and depended on him to a large extent. But he had also to depend on the help and good will of the Europeans, who would undoubtedly have cut him dead had he started "fraternizing" with his servant.

The unstinting hospitality so often offered Ivan by the latter, often on no warning at all, was undoubtedly due in part to letters of introduction—his mother had visited the then East Indies some years before—and in part to Ivan's own charm. One of the masters at Eton had remarked somewhat plaintively that Ivan got away with things that would have sent other boys to the headmaster's office. Too, the rather isolated Europeans were inclined to pounce on anyone who could bring them news from home, not so much political or social (in the broader sense), but the ordinary gossip of the day. News traveled more slowly in those days (airmail was extended to Java only in 1933), and anyone recently arrived from Europe—or other parts of the East Indies—particularly a well-educated and charming young man with known "good connections," was welcomed with open arms by British and Dutch alike. His letter of introduction from the British Museum, of course, stood him in good stead with the scientists.

If some of Ivan's ideas seem naïve—and there are blatant gaps apparent in his knowledge—bear in mind that he was only seventeen when he set out and had not yet gone to a university. Officially, natural history was given very short shrift at Eton, and though they were sympathetic to his interest in this field, there was hardly a master or a tutor who did not at one time or another suggest that it would be helpful if he paid more attention to the required studies. He was not, I am afraid, a very good student, and even his own excursions into natural history had been somewhat erratic and undirected.

Readers are warned that this account should not be taken as strictly "historical." Apart from those liberties I have already mentioned, there is always the chance that in some cases my memory of what Ivan told me may have played tricks on me. I hope, nonetheless, that it will prove enjoyable.

SABINA W. SANDERSON

Green
Silence

1

"The Place": The Jungle, What It Is, and How I Came to Be There

---

Ｉ F YOU HAVE EVER HAD THE luck to visit the great temple at Tel el Amarna in Egypt or even have seen photographs of it, with its close-packed ranks of great cylindrical columns placed so close together that from all but two angles you can't see through them, and if in your imagination you then litter its floor with a bumpy green carpet with black holes in it, and cap it with a soft, semiluminous mass of what looks like medicated cotton somewhere above which somebody has left lots of lawn sprinklers running at quarter pressure, you'll get as close a mental picture as I can give you of this place at dawn. Of course, the pillars here were not in neat ranks or all the same size, so you could not see through them for more than a certain distance in any direction. Westerners usually refer to it as looking like a cathedral, but I have never seen one almost completely filled with pillars, and the only place I know of that is, is the great Shinto temple at Nara in Japan, but the roof there is too low by about fifty feet.

This place was filled with an awe-inspiring kind of silence all its own, and this *was* cathedral-like, except that this silence was punctuated by a constant sound of dripping water from above and occasional splashings that emanated from the black holes in the green-manteled carpet, and from deep down in them moreover, so that the whole place really sounded like a gigantic bathroom of some kind. So saturated was the air in there that it shimmered, giving much the same effect as if seen through a florist's window down the inside of which a fine film of water is arranged to fall evenly all along. Thus, both sight and sound were really quite unearthly and, had I then heard of science fiction or read any, I might well have felt that I had stepped through some sort of time warp into another universe; moreover, the stepping had been just about as abrupt as going through an airlock, having been not more than a dozen paces from the more normal world outside, which I shall describe later.

Of course, I knew that the pillars were trees going straight up, but they had not a leaf on them until they vanished into the mist above. They were all wet, with here and there tiny rivulets running down the bark, and they looked black. The floor of this place was passing strange. It was entirely composed of enormous fallen tree trunks in various stages of rot and piled higgledy-piggledy at all angles and in disordered layers going on down about thirty feet where, as I found later by peering down into the black holes, they lay in still, dark waters. They were all themselves carpeted with mosses, ferns, and other lowly plants that in the dim light could be seen to be green, but now in the lowest key.

I was careful not to go too far into this incredible place, because it looked the same in all directions and seemingly went on forever, and, as I found out later, it more or less did, comparatively speaking. Keeping a keen eye on my bearings from the point where I had entered, I crept cautiously along the great moss-covered logs for not more than about a couple of hundred feet, and then I squatted down to listen to the silence. Drip, drip, drip; and every now and then this sudden splashing below. I peered down one of the black holes, and as it got a little lighter, I could see the jet-black waters swirl momentarily; then silence again. Nothing else. It was eerie but not frightening; an almost unbelievable world of mystery and also majesty. I felt that I had stepped back in time, and in a way I had, for I learned later that the fallen trees that lay all about must have fallen hundreds or thousands of years before to make room for the closely packed giants that grew up among them as grass might do through a grill. And I just sat, waiting for what I really did not know, but waiting nonetheless, and with an ever mounting expectancy.

Dawn comes abruptly at six on the equator. It was now seven o'clock and I could vaguely hear noises from "outside." The sun was well up out there but it had not yet penetrated this place, except to flood it with its strange, almost luminous gray half-light. The only thing to which I can liken this diffused light is eclipses of the sun as one enters the penumbra. It's an eerie sort of light without any of the red end of the spectrum. No shadows, and something wrong with close distances.

But now something *was* happening, but so gradually it was almost imperceptible. Light was getting in from above so that the green ground (if you could call it that) cover was becoming ever brighter. This continued very slowly until it became iridescent, due, I perceived, to every tiny leaf being as if sprayed with tiny droplets of water. Then, about the time I had to leave—for the very mundane reason of common courtesy to my host, whom I had only met the night before and who obviously had a rather rigid regime for feeding times—the mist above suddenly thinned out and true sunlight came in, though completely filtered, so that one could have imagined that somebody had turned on a gigantic, bright-green neon light somewhere above. The expectancy was suddenly fulfilled. As I got up to leave, one great bird let out a screech that echoed through the place just as it would have in an enormous cathedral. Then silence again until I had stepped out of the place, crossed a small ravine, and set out across half a mile of cleared higher land to the estate house where I had been asked to be by eight sharp if I wanted breakfast.

Here I should like to go back and tell you how I got where I was. I am going to make this rather brief except for the last lap of my journey, which was to me more than interesting to say the least. However, even this did not prime me for my experience that morning, but it was truly the start of my education and the introduction to the life I had so steadfastly decided to follow.

I was born in Edinburgh, Scotland, but I always hated

the north and the climate, and the people for that matter, and all I ever wanted was to get to the tropics. It was Alfred Russel Wallace who started me off, particularly with his book entitled *The Malay Archipelago,* which I was given when I was a really little one. I had read other bits and pieces and looked at pictures, but from Wallace's book I got confirmation of what I had always believed about the tropics.

I managed to pass some examination at my so-called public school—which is, of course, a private school— actually Eton, when I was sixteen, some kind of examination called "higher certificate," which you are not supposed to even try to get until you are at least seventeen, but I managed somehow. I don't know how, because I was always bottom of the class and I was lazy and incredibly stupid,* but I managed to get five credits—in what departments I don't know, but never mind. I got loose, and that meant that I could apply for sponsorship to go to a university, specifically Cambridge, though I did a bit of wangling there, because my house master at Eton, old C. J. M. Adie, Esq., a hard-boiled Scot, who was alleged to be the only Britisher who ever spoke French with a

---

*For those who may look on this statement as either false modesty or inverse exaggeration, it is neither. Of the reports from Eton, C. J. M. Adie wrote Ivan's mother: "The enclosed reports, though not actively abusive, are disappointing; . . . I am all for encouraging his interest in Natural History as a side line; but I am inclined to fear that he is allowing it to take up too much of his attention, to the exclusion of the to him duller but more immediately pressing subjects. . . ." And his mathematics tutor noted that "He is no sort of trouble in School, but I should welcome a less limp attitude to things in general." He was not, in these reports, absolutely bottom of the class, but he came close. [S. W. S.]

French accent,* sponsored me to go to Cambridge. He couldn't stand the sight of me—I *was* a blasted nuisance, and I know it—but he must have seen beyond what I was then, because he did sponsor me. This meant that I ought to have taken another examination, which is called "little-go," but everybody cheated everybody else, because I went off on this trip just before my seventeenth birthday. I told Mr. Adie that if he would send the papers to me in Japan I would be happy to take the examination under supervision. Well, we British are not so utterly stupid, and it was all neatly arranged that I never had to take the damned thing and I wasn't in Japan at the time anyhow, so I went to Cambridge sponsored, without having to take another examination. But that is future history.

Just before my fourteenth birthday my mother somehow got me into Eton; no one ever knew how she managed it, but then, she was an extraordinary person. She now gave me a choice: to go straight on to Cambridge, or to take the £500 left me by my father and travel around the world. In fact, she made it fairly clear that she preferred the latter course, since I had clearly "to learn the value of money." The rules were simple. I had to cross the international dateline, which lies at the opposite side of the earth from my point of departure, which was actually Greenwich in London. If then still alive and (rather obviously) out of cash, I was to get the cost of steerage passage home to England on arrival on the west coast of America. So I went off from England with some tin trunks full of all the wrong things, by train

*If Ivan's imitation was accurate, he wasn't and he didn't. [S. W. S.]

to Folkestone, from there to Boulogne, and then across France to Marseilles where I went aboard a ship called the *City of Baroda.* I grew very fond of that ship.

There were about twenty passengers; otherwise the *City of Baroda* was a sort of local freighter, stopping at every possible port all the way through the Suez Canal and on across to India, Ceylon, and finally Malaya, to take on and discharge cargo. In a number of cases we had time to go ashore, sometimes for several days, catching the steamer at its next port, which I did in order to see Egypt, but I am not going to detail these visits here —they have nothing to do with jungles, and it is the latter that I want to tell you about.

It is probably a useless exercise, but I shall repeat myself anyway.*

Our word "jungle" is derived from a Persian name for a certain kind of very small and usually thorny scrub that covers the deserts between the true sandy and stony wastes and the nearest vegetation having massed shrubs or scattered trees—namely what is properly called the Orchard Bush in the tropics. The Persian word for this is *djanghael.*

This word was introduced into India by the early British political officers, who spent much of their time hunting. There was *djanghael* aplenty in the drier parts of northern India, and there was the hunting they knew in Persia—gazelle and other antelope, and so on.

As British influence spread in India, it penetrated successively the Orchard Bush, and then the various

---

*See *Ivan Sanderson's Book of Great Jungles* (Simon and Schuster), for example.

belts of farmed, tertiary, and secondary forest until it finally entered what is called the Tall Equatorial Deciduous Evergreen Closed-Canopy Forests. By a mere act of fate and because there was no other ready term for places to hunt, the term "jungle" went along with this expansion.

Now, in those days there were no sciences of vegetalogy (the way plants grow and the kind of growth they produce) or phytogeography (the mapping of the distribution of specific plants, their genera, families, etc.), and no distinction was made even between the Scrublands bordering deserts and the drier forests. It was recognized that there was something else, sort of "beyond" this, that was composed of perpetually green (even if each tree was deciduous at some time during the year), perpetually moist forests of great size and having a sort of roof over them composed of their main foliage. There was no name for this but, since it was a forest like the tertiary and secondary forests, it was at first dubbed simply more "jungle."

It was Rudyard Kipling who first really muddled the issue, though he never actually implied or included the closed-canopy forests in his "jungle" books, simply because he never went there and seems not to have known just what they were like and how they differed from his "jungles." It was left to Edgar Rice Burroughs to bring on the real semantic muddle. He put Jane and Tarzan in what was very nearly real closed-canopy forest—at least the film sets show large trees and creepers and vines standing quite close together—and he called this the Jungle, at first implying and then pounding it in for sixty years, that any and all types of tropical forest with trees are jungles. As a result, the original Persian word for desert scrub ended up as the only recognized term for the equatorial closed-canopy forests, and there is nothing that I or anyone else can ever do that will pry the general public loose from this notion.

The trouble here is that the closed-canopy forests—properly called the Tall Equatorial Deciduous Closed-Canopy Forests and the Tall Equatorial Evergreen Closed-Canopy Forests (TED and TEE for short)—are totally distinct from all other types of forests, tropical or otherwise, and the latter is greatly more distinct than is the former. One cannot call all these forests, even the tropical ones, by the same name, while the name "jungle" is least appropriate to the TED and the TEE for two reasons. First, it is the farther from the Persian desert scrub; and, secondly but much more important, what people have been conditioned to call the true jungle (i.e., the TED and TEE) is not at all what they have been led to suppose through sixty years of books, articles, and films. No film has ever been made in the true closed-canopy forests. It can't be done, both from the technical point of view and the fact that there is nothing to see therein except at night or two hundred feet above your head.

The net result of all of this is that people talk endlessly of going on safaris to the "jungles" of East Africa or northeast India, where there is not and never has been so much as a patch of this TEDECCF. Everybody is, of course, perfectly happy as they are after big game and photography, and this goes for government persons and businessmen and everybody else quite apart from tourists. They've got the wrong name first off and they certainly don't know the difference, and I have finally come to realize that nobody really knows what it is or even where it is. This suits me fine, as I shall be only too happy if they keep their cotton-picking fingers off it and out of it.

Needless to say, I did not know all this when I set off, and had to unlearn all that I had been taught. Though I shall surrender to popular usage and employ the word jungle, I hope that by the time you have finished this book, you will have some notion of just what the true "jungle" is.

2

---

*The Outward Journey and a Visit to
Ceylon; The Slender Loris*

I
T GOT VERY HOT AND DRY
rather suddenly when we went through the Straits of Bab
el Mandeb. Then we turned around into the Bay of
Aden, which is on the southeast face of Arabia. I suppose
I should have gone ashore; anybody who had the chance
to see Aden in 1928 ought to have taken it, but you don't
do everything. And I had been up most of the night
talking with a retired engineer I had met on deck. He had
worked for various companies and the British Colonial
Government and was now going back around the world
from Britain via various places where he had lived, then
to America and on across the Atlantic to England. He
was probably in his late sixties and had spent almost his
entire life in the tropics. He proved to be an amateur
astronomer and, since we were beginning to see the

Southern Hemisphere, he told me all about the stars and galaxies and so on, and we forgot about the time.

The boat stayed at Aden only one day and then headed out into that loveliest of all seas, the Arabian. It was as smooth as the proverbial millpond, with thousands of flying fishes and, at night, great sheets of phosphorescence. This last was produced by the little *Noctiluca miliaris,* which were apparently stirred up by great numbers of squid going backward. The sea birds were unbelievable—this was over a hundred miles from the nearest land—and as a novice naturalist, I just gawped at all of this. The engineer, the Hindu doctor, and a woman—I can't remember who she was*— and I made up a sort of coterie on deck, both day and night, and I profited greatly from this. They were all very knowledgeable and intelligent and did all they could to prepare me for my stay in the East Indies.

We were about two hundred miles from land—a sparkling, windless day—when we suddenly began to be aware of the most extraordinary scent on the air: a mixture of burning rosewood, all the makings of a curry, and other less definable fragrances. I said, "But this smells marvelous; what is it?" The engineer and the doctor both chuckled and one of them, I forget whom, said, "Well, there's no wind actually, but there is a wind drift, and that, my boy, is the smell of the tropics." And it was.

Our first stop was at Bombay, and I got up at six o'clock and dressed in a great hurry in order that I might get off on the first land leg of my trip, intending to go

---

*Probably a Dr. (Miss) Lambert, with degrees in physiology and an expert on the thymus gland. [S. W. S.]

by train across India to Madras and then on to Ceylon. Alas, we were not allowed to land at all because of cholera on shore, only those passengers specifically booked for Bombay (including the doctor) being taken off. So I had to content myself with a short visit to India much later.

It was a lovely hot day—the humid heat of the tropics that lays out most Westerners but that I revel in—and the huge expanse of Bombay harbor looked very lovely, shrouded in smoky mist from the town, with the brownish sea and pinkish rocky crags on the southern side, and tall palm trees silhouetted against the gray-blue sky. The sun was so bright that it looked as if a cloud was just going to pass over it.

I did some drawing in the morning and watched the Tamil coolies loading our cargo and sleeping in the sun. They came alongside in marvelous dhow-shaped boats but with more beam, using thin bamboos as boathooks. These Tamils are for the most part copper colored and wore the most extraordinary variety of clothing, everything from a mere loincloth to frock coats. They were reasonably efficient, though, and we sailed shortly after noon for Ceylon.

It would be difficult to choose a more striking introduction to the wonderland of the Far East than Ceylon [see Figure 3], justly called the Eden of the Eastern Seas. The *City of Baroda* was scheduled to stop at Colombo for a week, a fact I checked carefully with the captain to avoid being left or nearly left behind as on previous occasions, and I was thus able to do some real "exploring."

We arrived at Colombo at about five o'clock and got ashore about half an hour later. It is a most gorgeous place, a large, straggling town with lovely bungalows and modern buildings interspersed with waving tall palms and wonderful tropical trees. We went ashore in a motor tender that came alongside covered with very clean, neat-looking coolies in khaki and some in sailor suits (the harbor police). Everything in the harbor was almost excessively neat and orderly, and there was no pushing of boats at the gangway. The boats were tied to buoys in two or three long rows pointing seaward, and the outer harbor was very spacious and enclosed by artificial walls.

Getting on shore, we passed through many spotless sheds and by jetties and eventually came out by the Grand Oriental Hotel. I went off by myself and bought some cigarettes, but later met a couple from the boat who very kindly took me for a drive all around the town. We went through the large Malay section of Colombo, down a street just wide enough for two cars and crowded with men. The shops were all open, and there was no pavement. Several phonographs were going with recordings of Indian music, and everywhere swarms of men and children gossiping, laughing, and singing. Some wore sarongs but most a white loincloth and a white shirt, or a form of white Arab getup. Several important-looking, stout men carried umbrellas, which looked most absurd on a warm, starry night with crickets and cicadas buzzing everywhere and the air alive with fireflies.

The next morning, feeling that I must not waste another moment in getting on with my objective of collecting animals, I invested in a stout knapsack and the equipment necessary for catching and preserving insects and small mammals, and then hired a taxi to drive me into the uninhabited low country covered with palm growth. The driver did not understand English so, after filling up with gasoline, he called for an interpreter. Luckily a dear little Singhalese came up and, on discovering what I wanted, immediately offered to come and "do bearer" for me, so I engaged him, and away we went at top speed. Our driver, Sammy, was very good, and although the roads were filled with people, oxcarts, trucks, cars, rickshaws, and animals, we never hit anything. We went north toward Kadawella through a most interesting part of the town. The road was good and very straight and banded by palm trees, native shops, and little gardens, and all covered with wonderful exotic vegetation and bathed in glowing sunlight. The natives mostly wear white cotton cloth, though the high-caste Singhalese wear white silk jackets decorated with red braid and glistening brass buttons and a sort of sarong, often a gay plaid, and the Buddhist priests are everywhere in their orange togas.

As we got into the country, the houses grew fewer and fewer. They were, however, often very neat and airy, being a bungalow with verandah and windows and a little garden in front. Some, it is true, were mere huts, but almost all were built of native bricks, which are very regular but sandy; no mortar is used. All along the road we passed men and women carrying wares on their heads. The men were mostly thin but not at all badly built; the women very upright, well covered, and, as we got into the country, remarkably beautiful. I afterward learned from my bearer that those in the town are nearly all "sick" (evidently riddled with venereal disease), whereas the country folk are entirely free from it. Two-wheeled carts covered with a palm-thatch hood and drawn by one or two tiny humped oxen seemed to be the chief method of transport.

We stopped at one place and collected several fine butterflies and then drove on to another spot where we descended to a river, or rather a river valley, where there was a native brickyard. My bearer enquired of the workers for birds and mammals, but none were obtainable, so we backtracked to the road and then walked in about a mile to a small native village. Here I was given a fresh coconut to drink while my bearer again explained my needs. Off they went with dogs and sticks, and back they came bearing lizards, toads, huge grubs, and a variety of bugs. One Agamid lizard they caught in about five minutes by means of a grass noose and a bent stick. The lizard was a sandy color with darker-brown markings and a slight crest above the neck. It had a way of sitting up on its front legs and down on the hind legs, much like a dog sitting on its haunches.

Soon there appeared a large hairy man in a loincloth who said he knew of two very rare animals that he would get and send to his cousin who worked at the Grand Oriental Hotel, promising that these would arrive before eight thirty that evening. He wrote his cousin's name, but in English, and since it was "William," it didn't help much. And when we returned to the hotel, nothing happened, so I went back to the boat for the night.

This very short "cruise" was not without incident and was in fact rather hilarious. I had missed the official tender and, along with several others in the same situation, had to bargain with one of the Singhalese. There were some dozen liners in the roads, and it was eventually agreed that we should make a round trip, depositing and taking aboard people from all of them. We all climbed into the launch.

Now amongst our number was a large, perspiring lady obviously hailing from the United States, who was festooned like a Christmas tree with concrete testimonies of the persuasiveness of the Singhalese and her own gullibility. No sooner were we in the launch than she started fussing and worrying about her boat, which she told us was on a round trip and due to leave any minute. At each stop she made frantic efforts to disembark but compassionate hands held her back.

Finally we came to a towering liner, blowing loudly, her anchor winches creaking and sailors pulling on the ropes of the gangway. The dear old soul was beside herself with terror and nearly fell out of the boat waving to her husband on the deck far above. We came alongside just as the gangway was starting to go aloft. Everybody helped; we lifted her bodily over the space between the boat and the ship; we gathered up her countless geegaws and passed them over. We were all greatly amused watching her clamber laboriously up the steep steps. At the top she billowed into the arms of several stewards. The liner was gathering speed fast, headed for the open ocean. The last we saw of her she was gesticulating wildly amid a large crowd on the deck. Then the Singhalese turned the launch to the next boat.

Two humorless Britishers came aboard and took up their positions on the seat lately vacated by our American friend. I heard a slight commotion at their end of the launch and craned over to see what it was.

"Excuse me," drawled one of the Englishmen, "But does anybody own this?"

He held up a large purse. We looked at each other.

"Good Lord! I believe that belongs to the old American geezer," somebody said, and when it was ascertained that it belonged to none of us, it was agreed that we should examine its contents.

It belonged to her all right. There was a passport and a little money and a green landing card. On that card was inscribed the name of a well-known British liner bound from Europe to Shanghai that was placidly riding at anchor not three hundred yards away. Everybody gasped and with one accord looked out to sea. Almost on the horizon now was the French vessel that the poor lady had so laboriously boarded.

"Great Scott!" a small man shouted. "That boat she's on is bound for Europe. Its next port of call is Mauritius. I've just left the captain."

I have often wondered what happened to the poor thing; the world is such a big place for old ladies without luggage or passport.

The next morning I went back to the hotel to see if the animals had arrived, but they had not, nor could the cousin be found. I then found my driver Sammy and my "bearer," who promptly announced that we should go to Kandy, the capital of Ceylon. This is up in the mountains and is, I suppose, one of the most beautiful places in the world. There were hotels, government offices, and such, and all the white officials used to spend most of their time up there; but it was the gardens all around it that were absolutely fabulous. They had all kinds of things that I had never really seen before, palms of all kinds, fern trees, and all these beautifully tended lawns with flowering bushes. It was almost unbelievable to me. Then you had the most marvelous views all around, and all framed by flowering plants, all the way from lowly herbs to giant trees.

My "bearer" determined that I should have the Grand Tour of Kandy and took me to the Temple of the Tooth, a time-worn structure built of gray stone, rather simple in its architecture and set in a lotus grove on the shores of a crystal-clear lake. I was told that one of the Gautama Buddha's teeth, found in Burma, is preserved here, but I did not see it. Apparently it is kept inside a maze of boxes and displayed on only the most special occasions to persons who have proved themselves sympathetic to Buddhism (I would have passed muster here), in a ceremony accompanied by what the Singhalese consider music. My engineer friend later informed me that "There are two simple rules governing the production of Singhalese music: first, make as much noise as possible all the time; second, to enhance the effect, make more."

For some reason Sammy, the taxi driver, decided (despite our lack of any common language) that I should dine with some relatives of his, and this was explained to me by my bearer. Having been initiated into the niceties of Eastern table manners by my teachers on the *City of Baroda* and the pleasures of a good curry by my mother, I accepted with alacrity. Whether any of us were expected I have never been certain, but the lady of the house never even blinked at the sudden additions at her table, and the curry was excellent but served without any table utensils. Here etiquette demands that you dig a hole in the center of the mound of rice on your plate, dump the various curries into this excavation and mix thoroughly. Then, without bending a joint of the hand, plunge it into the mixture, draw the fingers together and finally suck the food off them. It is more than ill-bred to eat from the palm of the hand.

It was after dinner that I discovered the real reason for this visit. I was taken into the garden behind the house where they had, not quite as a pet, a Slender Loris (*Loris tardigradus*). These are inhabitants of southern India and Ceylon, where they live in the trees of the low-lying forests, though they are now quite common on estates and gardens around houses. The coat displays that peculiar range of colors found among the lemurs and is also rather like that of the Kinkajou with its lights and shades and bright sheens. The general effect is a yellowish gray, but all over the back there is a reddish tinge together with a silvery wash, while the inside of its limbs and belly are lighter, and the legs, where the fur is naturally somewhat parted, show dark gray, the color of the base of the hairs. The Slender Loris [see Figures 4 and 5] of Ceylon is distinctly lighter than that found on the Indian continent. The eyes are enormous and placed very close together, and there is a narrow white stripe between the eyes that spreads out on the forehead and finally fades away above. The animal is only about eight inches long, much smaller than its cousin the Slow Loris (*Nycticebus coucang*).

It is quite impossible to hurry the Slender Loris. Even when frightened it moves along in the most ridiculously precise and careful way, never releasing its hold on one branch with more than one hand or foot at a time and making certain that three are firmly "glued" to the next branch before finally shifting the final hand or foot. It seems to be true that by this excessive stealth these animals really can creep up on sleeping birds and catch them by slowly grasping the wretched creatures before they know what has happened. When they have a bird in their hands they proceed to pluck it just as we would a chicken, and then tear up the body and munch away contentedly until the meal is finished. The Slender Loris is not, however, entirely a bird eater, feeding also on insects, fruits, young shoots, some leaves, and birds' eggs when it can find them. Sammy provided an egg for their resident loris, and it proceeded to break it by squeezing it between its chin and its chest, unlikely as this may sound.

These animals move about by night and can apparently see perfectly well in the dark. During the day they sleep rolled up in a ball with their heads between their thighs and their feet firmly anchored to some suitable branch. They are mysterious, quiet creatures but they can make the night horrible with long plaintive cries that seem to come from nowhere in particular. They produce only one baby at a time, which they carry about with them and look after very carefully.

The Singhalese collect the huge eyes of the Slender Loris and use them as charms, in love potions, and particularly to make medicines for the cure of eye diseases.

I made a half-hearted attempt to buy this animal, but it was clear that it was not really for sale. On the other hand—and this was actually most mysterious—they brought out a number of small bamboo cages containing

Black Rats *(Rattus rattus rattus),* but of all shapes, sizes, and colors, and indicated that these were a gift. Now, my basic objective was to collect rats of all kinds throughout the Orient, and I eventually acquired about forty subspecies. These first specimens proved to be very valuable because the Black Rat, carrier of bubonic plague among other things, is an arboreal animal and an Oriental animal. There is a black variety that got into Europe quite early on, but normally the "Black Rat" is not black. One of these collected at Kandy was a beautiful reddish brown with bright yellow beneath the head and body and inside the limbs, while another was a slaty blue-gray, lighter beneath and almost black on the back.

I took these rats back to the ship, where I killed them with the help of the ship's doctor and then skinned and stuffed them. This was a business I was just learning, and it is a bit ticklish. My intent was what are called "flat specimens," with their little front paws pinned up by their ears and the back ones backwards. The tail is the major difficulty. The bone and meat are drawn out of the tail and then a wire wrapped in cotton wool painted with arsenical soap is inserted. You have to learn how to roll enough but not too much. If you've got too much, of course it won't go in, and if you have too little, the tail will shrink around it and look horrible. However, I got all this done and crated them up and shipped them home.

I still had several days in Ceylon, and on the advice of a British resident to whom I had a letter of introduction, I rounded up Sammy, who took me on what was then a day's drive to the Sinharaja Forest. This was my first sight of a closed-canopy equatorial forest. There were three or four tiers of trees, and the top ones were at least two hundred feet high; the next tier underneath that was, I would say, about a hundred feet high, and then there was about a fifty-foot tier and a few saplings underneath, but you could have ridden a bicycle through it. There were no roads into it then, and you had to go in on foot. I did not penetrate very far and arrived, though I did not realize it then, at the dead time of day. I saw a few insects but apart from these, nothing, not even a solitary bird. Like probably everyone else, I had grown up with the idea that jungles were concentrated zoological gardens with animals cavorting all over the place. What I had seen of nonjungle tropical woodlands and other types of growth had certainly encouraged this notion, since there seemed always to be a multitude of life, even if only birds, in sight. Nevertheless, this short visit impressed me deeply, though it did not in fact prepare me for what lay ahead.

3

Malaya: Of Salamanders and Other Breakfast Marvels, and the Kaguan

THE GULF OF BENGAL IS UT-
terly different—at least it was in those days—from the
Arabian Sea on the other side. It was absolutely blank
until we got into the string of islands—the Andamans
and the Nicobars—and had to pass between them to go
to the Malacca Straits and Pinang. This channel is really
quite wide; you can't see either the southernmost Anda-
man Island nor the northernmost Nicobar, but it sort of
shelves off, and then you turn into the Malacca Strait.

I was up but not yet on deck when a steward, an English Cockney, came to my cabin and said, "I think you'd
like to see this, sir; come and I'll show you something."
I followed him up, not knowing what to expect, though
I knew that word had got around about my being a naturalist and interested in any kind of animal life. It was a

/ 25

perfect sunny day without any clouds in the sky, and although the sea should have been completely calm, it was "boiling." This was caused by what appeared to be millions of sea snakes mating. The steward told me that they came across this every year at this time and that the sea snakes seemed to cover an area some two miles wide and as much as fifty long. These snakes are called *kraits* (pronounced *krīte*) and are deadly poisonous. Their tails are flattened, up and down, not top and bottom, and there are dozens of species, all wildly colored: black and red, black and yellow, iridescent blue and green, and what have you. I was to meet them at closer range later while traveling from Bali to the Celebes by native prau.

The *City of Baroda* finally dumped me off at a place called Port Wellesley, which is on the mainland opposite the island of Pinang on the west coast of what was then called the Malay States. I crossed to the island to stay a week with an old friend of an uncle of mine who had spent most of his life in Sumatra, where this gentleman had also lived before his semiretirement. Then I crossed back to the mainland, heading for a rubber estate way up in the back of the State of Perak. I did not go back to Port Wellesley but to a tiny place by the name of Burak, which was really only a sort of landing stage for local traffic to a town some miles inland called Bukit Merjatam. This consisted of a cluster of warehouses, some small docks, and a roadhead. On this road there were lined up a rank of large open American touring cars, mostly Packards, polished to mirror gloss, and each containing two men. The non-drivers were all standing on their running-boards with raised arms, waving and shouting. These were taxicabs. European cars, short of Rolls-Royces, just would not run in the tropics in those days because they had been invented in and devised for a European climate; American cars, on the other hand, were both bigger and sturdier and had been manufactured to cope with a very wide range of climates, including such places in the tropics as Panama and Puerto Rico. There being no tourists or tourist agents in that place at that time, one made one's own arrangements with the *seises* (pronounced *sy-ces*) or owner-drivers of these polished cars, and it was a matter of hard bargaining. Luckily, I had had some experience of this in the eastern Mediterranean, and it was one of my favorite hobbies, so on this occasion I had my rather mountainous baggage dumped on the road halfway up the line and settled down to indulge a happy time.

There were more than a dozen cars in this static parade, all but four driven by pairs of Malays. Three of the others were owned by Tamil Indians, and one by a lone Chinese gentleman of rather monumental proportions dressed in a natty white business suit, white shirt, black tie, and topped off with a straw boater of the Harold Lloyd type, tipped to a jaunty angle. At first I thought that he was alone, but as I moved down the line a really minute replica of this distinguished Far Easterner bobbed up in the driver's seat. He did not look more than twelve years old. Bargaining was sprightly once these assorted vultures got over their surprise at meeting a Britisher who not only expected to have to bargain but who apparently relished it. Convincing them of this was achieved only by my calling the two dockers who had toted my baggage and who were hanging around to watch the fun, and offering them a more than modest sum to return my loads to the dock to await the next ferry. That sort of broke the dam and, of course, not a suitcase was touched. I provided a local coconut soft drink, in rather dirty glasses, bought from a little wheel-cart tended by a very ancient Indian, and settled down to business. It turned into a sort of auction in reverse.

I wanted to go really rather a long way, for those days, into the outer limbo of the next State, Perak, through some mountains far to the east and this, combined with the fact that I had of course never been there before, made bargaining a bit difficult. In the Near East you cut the asking price to an eighth if you are not particularly interested and a sixth if it is essential. I compromised for a seventh but these boys were awfully tough, and it was half an hour before one offered two-thirds. Then the fun began, because I got them bargaining among themselves even to the use of their cars. I should explain that none of these were paid for. The importers rented them out for a minimum payment per day, and cancellation of agreement or much worse if the car was so much as scratched; no insurance you understand. The poor boys just had to get the dealer's price as it were—except for the Chinese gentleman. He owned his car outright, as I found out later; his driver was his minute son and was not paid; and he was insured in Singapore. So, of course, when he had seen enough of the fun and no other cus-tomers had loomed up, he offered me a price that under-cut all the others by half. It was then that I first learned why the Malays were not too fond of the Chinese.

Most of the morning having been spent in this exer-cise, the small driver tended to hurry, and even then we did not roll in until after dark. Incidentally, it turned out that the Chinese gentleman just happened to be under contract with the estate cook for the supply of all victuals! Coincidence perhaps? Anyhow, he lived in the nearest village at that end, only some twenty miles away, and I do not think that he was normally in the jockey business but knew of my arrival via the grapevine. He was an absolutely splendid chap and gave up being the inscrutable Oriental as soon as we had roared out of town in a cloud of fine dust. From then on he talked almost as much as I did—and it is alleged that I was talking before I was born—and graciously accepted my invitation to come sit with me in the back seat. This made shouting easier, and I knew he would have been of no use up front in case of extreme emergency, as any Chinese behind the wheel of a car in the tropics is just as terrifying as any other; and praying doesn't do any good either. But the poor chickens.

Mr. (and please not to forget it) Chung Se'i Gon was also a very civilized man, I soon discovered. I don't know if he had traveled, but he knew the difference between an upper-, a middle-, and a lower-class Englishman, and when I told him that I didn't trust any white man, he really opened up and started twitting me about "Honest John Chinamen," which tickled him no end. He leaned heavily toward the political but never really mentioned the British government. His *bêtes-noires* were the merchants and petty officials who were, of course, mostly very middle class and appalling. He gave me to understand that he liked the Malays but had an utter contempt for their calculated laziness and rather puffy superiority complex—actually my impression is that they would rather be happy and independent than rich. The Indians he just plain despised, but those in that area were almost all poor Tamils. And I'll never forget his summation of the Levantines: "Rather good businessmen but terribly dishonest." But I think he was bolstering the "Honest John" bit. Nonetheless, he made a charming companion on the long drive and told me lots of things about the country that I wanted to know.

My host at the estate, to whom I had sent a letter of introduction in advance, was quite a different sort though he looked almost as Chinese as Mr. Chung, but was as svelte as the latter was blubbery. They treated each other with very good manners and mutual deference, I noted. My host was, I knew, the product of an actual marriage (not just a liaison) between a rather wealthy Scots aristocrat and a very high-class northern Chinese lady from Shantung. He had, of course, been educated in Europe but no longer left the Orient. He was a senior manager for the British firm of Harrison & Crossfields, who owned rubber, tobacco, and other plantations throughout Malaysia, which covers what was then the Dutch East Indies, now Indonesia.

As I have said, it was well after sundown when we arrived, and the night was moonless and overcast by what I later learned was the high mist that formed as the sun went down. Since it had got dark we had not seen a light along the road which meandered through tall forests as if through a canyon. Thus, coming to the estate house rather suddenly around a bend in the road was like approaching a liner on an open ocean at midnight. The estate house glowed internally with the soft golden light of oil lamps, and since there were windows all around the main part of the building, the outer walls of which opened onto the back of a wide verandah that ran all around, it looked like some kind of fairy palace that had suddenly popped up in the inky blackness of the night. And when the noise of the car engine was cut, the impression was enhanced by that silence that can only be truly achieved in the equatorial zones, a silence that is almost glutinous until your ears adjust to the fact that it is actually a colossal uproar caused by the insects, the frogs, and some others.

This estate house was comparatively new and had been built at the far end of an area selected for the estate before the general clearing started. It was near the eastern edge of a plateau clothed in dense forests of presumably secondary and with some tertiary growth, and it stood only about half a mile from its eastern boundary. This boundary was formed by a narrow but deep little ravine that formed a long bow from north to south. Beyond that ravine lay the tall equatorial forest. All around the estate house the land was in various stages of clearing and planting, there being left only a copse of shade trees around the house, and a considerable blob of mixed forest a mile to the northeast, in the cool shade of which a whole village had been built for the workers and the servants.

My host explained the layout in rough terms over dinner and, being very tired indeed from the trauma of Mr. Chung Junior's driving, I asked—as soon as it was polite to do so—to be permitted to go to bed and then to look around as soon after dawn the next morning as was possible. And that is how I got where I was before breakfast the next day.

As I walked back to the estate house across the cleared

land, I pondered what amounted to a couple of miracles, at least to me at that moment. The first was the marvel of the tall equatorial forest or so-called jungle itself, but the other more powerful emotion that almost over-stretched my belief in the orderliness of things was that I had hit my objective on my first try, and without the slightest indication from any source that I might do so. You see, the science of vegetalogy (i.e., the distribution of types of vegetation, *not* species) was then unborn, and tropical phytogeography (i.e., the distribution of plants themselves) was in its infancy, with only a tiny group of French, Dutch, British, and some German botanists and early forestry officers having even started such studies in the tropics. There were no vegetation maps, and the early foresters had not yet classified the various types of tropical growth and, more especially, those of the equatorial forests. Not even that marvelous place, the Map Room in the Royal Geographical Society in London, could tell me where the "jungle" was located and /or where it might still exist. People like my uncle who had lived in Sumatra most of his life and my host here who had been born in Malaya had not the foggiest notion what I was talking about. All they knew was that to clear land for plantations they required certain kinds of land and that it was useless trying to clear other kinds. Therefore I had no prior knowledge of what awaited me at this place. I could have missed the tall equatorial forest (TEF) by a hundred miles or by one mile. That I could walk for half an hour over cleared ground right to its edge on my first morning seemed then to me to be some-what miraculous. And, looking back on that morning from the vantage point of forty-five years, I perceive that there was another bit of serendipity there, for, of all the hundreds of true jungles, or TEFs, I have since visited, this one was the most staggering and the most classic, if I may so express this. Thus I was in somewhat of a daze when I sat down to breakfast.

My host was a saturnine man who adhered more than strictly to the old traditional ways, perhaps because of his "mixed" parentage. "Half-castes," as they were so disparagingly called by the pure Europeans, were given a very rough time socially in those days, and this often resulted in the male of the breed becoming aggressively traditional and in fact a snob. They were also awfully touchy and had a hidden hatred for pure whites, while they despised their mother's people. I had been warned of all this by a family friend who had given me a letter of introduction to that strange man, but I was considerably worried. At dinner the night before he had been frightfully formal, but now I found him awaiting me at breakfast in a trellised and vine-covered sort of arbor under the house, it being raised about eight feet off the ground, at a table spread with an immaculate white embroidered tablecloth and positively groaning with huge baskets of all kinds of fruits. I would not say that he was "relaxed"—a word that had not then been invented—but he was now considerably more human, dressed in khaki shirt and trousers and, I noticed to my delight, with bare feet.

This was particularly intriguing to me because it was one of the major medical shibboleths of those days that no white man should ever put his bare foot to the ground in the tropics, especially where local people (i.e., "natives") lived, because hookworm and some related types can enter the body through the skin of the feet. Thus, this sight presented me with a bit of a problem. However, after the formalities were over, I decided that the best thing to do would be to ask if I might take off my shoes and socks on the grounds that they were wet and were just plain hurting me. (Sneakers had not been invented in those days, and I still had not learned that tennis shoes, especially if stained brown or black, were the only possible thing to wear in any type of wild country unless you proposed to pound around after dark where there were poisonous snakes that hunt their prey by infrared or heat reception.) I had hit the right note, because my host said, "Certainly," and then, when I had done so and after looking at me in a rather strange way, he just put one of his feet up on the corner of the table. Nothing was said about hookworm.

It was that little incident, nonetheless, that broke the tension between us. In some way this strange, ostracized man appeared suddenly to have considered me as a human being—*his* kind of human being. He asked me where I had been and what I had been up to since dawn. I am afraid I became a bit effusive trying to explain all about jungles and TEF (tall equatorial forest), my curious lifelong (and it was then short enough indeed) desire to work in the latter, and how what I had seen that morning was to me the greatest stroke of luck I had ever had. He let me finish and then contemplated his papaya sprinkled with fresh lime juice and wild honey for a rather long time. His first remark was somewhat unexpected.

"I didn't know about all that," he said, and fell to further contemplation.

Knowing that I was a sort of super "bug hunter" and

an aspiring zoologist, he then started asking me all sorts of questions about the TEF and the fauna of his area. He was deeply interested in natural history but admitted with a sigh that he had never had time to pursue the matter. Nonetheless, he was a fund of information on the beliefs about them held by the locals. And these stories, I immediately perceived, were not all folklore or old wives' tales, something that present-day field naturalists, collectors, ethologists, and ecologists have still to learn. More success in my many years of subsequent fieldwork was derived from appreciating this fact—again so luckily and gratuitously handed to me at the outset of my career —than from anything else. When a person truly native to the country, not imported persons of other races or even other nearby tribes or nations, started to talk about the ways of *his* animals, I always listened attentively and respectfully, and I took notes. It depresses me to have to tell you that with but one or two exceptions those notes have always been refused for publication in learned journals; they were even eliminated from my huge catalogues of specimens collected. It wasn't until we turned up specimens of the mosquito that carries the most deadly form of cerebral malaria in a place where, according to medical people and entomologists, it should not have been, and a team from the Rockefeller Institute had made a search for it there, that somebody urged them to read my field notes. Then they found it breeding in wild bananas right under the houses they were living in!

Breakfast was further enlivened when I took a handful of small fruits onto my plate all at once; and out came a six-inch, shiny black wiggling something, the very existence of which I had never heard of. It was serpentine in

form but had a smooth skin and two small legs up behind
its head.

My host was so amazed that he literally yelled for the
head "boy" and started berating him even before he had
ended his lightning dash from somewhere abaft the
house. That such a thing should turn up on his breakfast
table he seemed to consider an outrage and, although I
could not understand a word he was saying, it was obvious from the increasing debility of said "boy" that he was
due for immediate "extinction." Meantime, I had
clamped an inverted tumbler over this wondrous thing
and was contemplating it with the utmost glee. Then, as
my host's tirade went on and other lesser minions were
called for questioning, I had a bright idea. I knew that
every detail of everybody new to anyplace in the tropics
is known to everybody there even before you arrive; and,
remembering what I had told the apparently omnipotent
Mr. Chung Senior the day before, I made a gallant effort
to come to the rescue of the head "boy," by asking my
host if he would tell him that I much appreciated this
thing as my first specimen.

I must say things got a bit complicated at that point.
My host was again aghast and obviously without words;
the head "boy" tried not to grin and succeeded with
quite extraordinary aplomb; the lesser lights literally
quivered with expectation; and I became very nervous
and started to try to explain myself with some fool rig-
marole about luck, happy coincidence, and, if I remember aright, I even dragged in Allah to try to explain the
incident. Finally, my host recovered and, with what I
could have sworn was a twinkle in his eye, dismissed the
shaking staff and remarked that in fact it must have been

the Will of Allah. But he then asked what the thing was and whether it lived inside fruits. Of course, I could not say, as I did not know what it was, and so I said that it looked like some kind of salamander and that I had never heard of any amphibian living *inside* fruit but that many did live among moist vegetation and thus possibly fruits. His reaction was typical. All he said was: "If my staff were going to waste their time and mine collecting your animals for you, I could have suggested a better way of presenting their first contribution." And there that matter ended, though I did notice that the staff were enormously solicitous of my welfare from then on.

This creature was indeed of the salamander order, but one of the strange group with only two legs, like our North American Congo Eels *(Amphiuma means)*. That specimen is somewhere in the vast collections of the British Museum in a bottle full of alcohol. I carried that bottle for over a year and delivered it in person instead of shipping it back as I did my other specimens from time to time. I suppose it acted as a sort of talisman, though I am not generally superstitious.

After this affair and when my host had gone off for his morning inspection, I had the time to myself until one o'clock (sharp, of course). I immediately set out for The Place again. But another strange event occurred. At various points along the cleared edge of the little ravine there were great piles of huge logs, the result of cutting up the giant trees that had fallen to that side. As I was circumnavigating one of these piles, I got a great shock when a mustachioed man brandishing a gleaming knife came sailing over the last log and landed almost at my feet [see Figure 7]. If I merely said I was scared, it would be to spoil the real effect, which was more of surprise. I didn't have time to think, and I believe that the man was as taken aback as I. He started stammering apologies in English, sheathed his knife, and gave a rather deep bow. I sort of did likewise, and when these preliminary amenities were over, I invited him to sit down on the log beside me. I was feeling rather weak.

It transpired that this man, Petros, was the headman for the rubber tappers and, like his boss, was also out on his morning round of inspection, which included land clearing, planting, and log burning. He had heard of my arrival but somehow had never expected to meet me wandering about alone in that area. He turned out to be a perfectly splendid chap and became my chief mentor. He had a most wonderful family and I fell for his number-two daughter the moment I laid eyes on her. Besides, his wife was the one who first taught me how to cook *nasi goreng*. He took every moment of his own time off to guide me about, instructing me in the art and the science of rubber tapping; and he showed me the local fauna, which he knew as well as any trained zoologist. The first example he produced for me that very morning by banging on a huge, dead, hollow tree standing on the edge of the jungle. Out popped one of the animals I most wanted to see in that area, called a Kaguan or Cobego (*Cynocephalus*). This creature needs a bit of explaining, because nobody has ever seemed to know quite what to do with it.

A corny old adage has it that a picture is worth a thousand words. Well, these [Figures 8 & 9] are going to have to serve for about three thousand. For the rest, I will endeavor to give a thumbnail sketch of these remarkable animals.

They live in the great forests of the Malay Peninsula, Siam, and the islands of Sumatra, Java, and Borneo, and there is another slightly smaller kind that inhabits the Philippine Islands. In those countries these animals are known by a variety of native names such as Kaguan, Colugo, Kubong, or Cobego, some of which are used by Europeans; and almost any Malay person will be able to describe this animal if you mention one of these names. There are only these two species of Kaguan, and there is no other animal at all like them anywhere else in the world, so that one naturally asks what they are and why they are so distinctive.

To answer the first question is not so easy because their brains are more like those of the Insectivores—the insect eaters, such as shrews, hedgehogs, and moles—whereas other parts of their bodies have led learned people to suppose that they are related to the lemurs or to the bats. An animal that links three such very different types of animal together must be unique, and this is the reason for their now being separated from all other mammals and placed in a special little Order of their own. They are called the *Dermaptera,* which means "skin-winged" and is a most sensible name, because stretched from either side of their necks is a thin flap of skin that gets wider and wider until it joins the thumb side of their hands. All the fingers are joined together by a web, and from the hinder edge of the hand these thin flaps of skin continue backward to the hind feet, which are also fully webbed. Finally, these flaps join the back legs to the tail, right to its tip, so that when a Kaguan opens its legs, spread-eagle fashion, it looks like a square kite and becomes a parachute. The skin flaps are covered with fur both above and below. They are nothing more than the ordinary body covering pulled out to form "planes," as in an airplane.

With the aid of these structures Kaguans glide about the forests at night. They "hobble" up to the tops of trees with some difficulty because their parachutes prevent their moving their limbs freely like other animals. When they are high enough up they leap out into the air, open themselves like kites, and go sailing away to some distant tree. If they begin to swerve around in the air, owing to a bad takeoff or air currents, they use their tails as rudders so that they get back onto their course and always make a perfect landing—and a perfect landing on the upright side of a tree trunk is not an easy thing to make. The flight of a Kaguan was once measured. It jumped from one tree and alighted on another two hundred and ten feet away. In this tremendous leap it descended only forty-two feet, showing that for every five feet that it traveled it dropped only one foot, which is about as good a performance as that of the paper darts we used to make at school. The strange parachutes and the gliding powers that they impart to their owners are, however, not the only things that make the Kaguans unusual.

Their lower front teeth are altogether remarkable, being like combs with lots of blade-shaped prongs packed together with their sharp edges all facing forward. Teeth like these are not to be found in any other mammal, though some poor imitations of them are seen in certain lemurs and, again, in an even more rudimentary state in some bats which have front teeth that are so heavily grooved up and down that it would require little more to turn them into tiny combs with a few "teeth." These teeth are undoubtedly used for combing the soft silky fur, but they also come in handy for biting or "sawing" off the tough leaves upon which Kaguans feed. Most of the unusual weapons and tools of animals are employed for more than one purpose.

Kaguans also have the beginnings of a second tongue underneath the ordinary one. Lemurs have this second, horny, stiff tongue, and it is used, among other things, for cleaning the hairs out of the front teeth. Lemurs, like the Kaguan, comb their fur with their lower front teeth and the loose hairs get wedged between them; then the animal puts its ordinary tongue out and over them; and, jamming its second hard tongue against the back of them, sucks upward sharply. The offending hairs are thus gripped as in a vise and so lifted out.

Altogether, what with their teeth and parachutes and several other things inside them, the Kaguans prove to be a unique offshoot of the mammalian tree of life. In one way, they may show how the bats were developed from ordinary little shrewlike insectivores that ran about the branches of trees many millions of years ago. In another way, or along another line of evolutionary development, with their large semiconvoluted brains and their second tongue, they would seem to point to the true Lemurs of Madagascar.

In color, the ordinary Kaguan exactly matches the bark of the tree boles and branches on which it spends most of its time. The fur of the back is olive-brown, sometimes with a slightly greenish tinge, and mottled with irregular white spots just like the lichen that grows on the trees. Underneath, there is a short thin fur, light brown in color but with a slightly reddish hue as if stained with tobacco juice. They are quite big animals, sometimes two feet in length, and the limbs are really very long and slender.

Kaguans are nocturnal and eat leaves, to digest which they have complicated, twisted stomachs. I once caught one of these animals in a hollow tree to which I was attracted by the most blood-curdling croaks, like a frog noise, only many times louder. This animal was a mother and was carrying two small naked babies that stuck flat against her chest and belly. They were blind and covered with wrinkles like dried-up old apples. These babies were probably twins, because Kaguans usually have only one baby at a time, to which they give birth while suspended upside down. Some Malay tribes believe that you cannot kill a Kaguan and that they are immortal. It is certainly true that they are one of the most difficult animals to kill; even the most dreadful accidents, causing wounds to the brain and spine that would be fatal to any other animal, do not kill them at once. Often they recover and get away when they have been left for dead.

The Kaguan that Petros produced came out of a large hole on the back of the tree and went humping up the main branch rather like a giant loop-caterpillar. I had a feeling that it was rather sleepy and resented being wakened to full daylight. When it got up about thirty feet, it paused and then turned around rather cumbrously until it was almost head downward, spread its front legs, gave a kick with its back legs, and sailed off into the jungle, which was only about fifty feet distant, and disappeared therein. Petros watched me with a curious expression. He could see that I was impressed, but I have a feeling to this day that he was rather annoyed that I knew what it was and could even put a name to it in his language. So I started asking a lot of questions. Perhaps the most interesting answer I got was that they normally sleep hanging upside down like bats, but in a ball, with head, shoulders, and tail rolled in and all four feet together on the branch above. The day before I left this place Petros took me out at dawn and showed me one hanging up-side-down, high up in a big leafy tree. We approached absolutely silently, but it took me about ten minutes to spot it, so perfectly camouflaged it was.

4

The Rhythm of the Jungle and Some Speculations on Jungle Growth

I LEFT PETROS THAT FIRST morning as he had work to do and he was very conscientious and, I believe, more than duly cognizant of his boss's ideas on due labor for just reward. Since it was after 11:00 A.M. when I left Petros and climbed down into the little ravine, I entered The Place at or rather in its Phase III, and thus became a bit confused and gained an entirely wrong impression of just what was what until Petros straightened me out a few days later. But let me try to explain this.

The twenty-four-hour day of the jungle is divided into seven unequal but clearly defined periods. There is manifestly a basic biorhythm here, but even after many years of firsthand experience, I cannot, of course, be sure that the divisions go as I list them below. And the "exact" timing must be arbitrary, and probably almost everybody who has not lived in the jungle for the express purpose of recording its bio-temporal rhythms will say that I am talking rubbish. However, you may by now know that I do not care one jot or tittle what they or anybody else says about this matter or anything else. Here are the facts laid out to the best of my ability and according to *our* time on the equator:

1) 5–8 A.M. (3 hours), Silence until sudden outburst.
2) 8–11 A.M. (3 hours), Uproar, decreasing to—
3) 11 A.M.–4 P.M. (5 hours), The Great Daytime Silence; then,
4) 4–6 P.M. (2 hours), Slowly increasing uproar leading to silence at sundown.
5) 6–11 P.M. (5 hours), Increasing noises; then sudden silence to—
6) 11 P.M.–2 A.M. (3 hours), The Great Nighttime Silence.
7) 2–5 A.M. (3 hours), Increasing noise, then fading to silence.

I had seen Phase I to its end—that first wild bird call —but then had missed the daily buildup due to all the breakfast, salamander, and meeting Petros bits. Thus I am going to ignore any actual chronology—some phases I did not see for many years and then thousands of miles distant, but the first three I did see here, so let me describe the second and third phases in order.

I entered the jungle, guided by Petros to start with, at 7:45 A.M. sharp. As before, the giant trees stood silent and weeping while the unseen canopy above dripped and things stirred in the black pools below. This time I went much farther in and Petros marked my path back out. He had also supplied me with my first machete. Again I sat down on one of the great logs and waited; and again came one lone, raucous screech from some great bird above the mists. Then, almost promptly at eight *"ack-emma,"* as we used to say, the great green neon light was turned on above, the mist vanished in minutes, and life began. It came slowly at first, with the bigger animals yelling back and forth at each other; but then the lesser ones began to join in, first above and then below. Here was an entirely new world, though one withal just as marvelous and in its quaint way mysterious.

It would take a Monet born in the tropics to capture the quality of the light in a jungle. Substantially, it is actually green but the air is so clear that it is absolutely transparent and the 100-percent humidity gives it a weird effect of what I can only describe as magnified nothingness—while it often does magnify. This is what defeats the photographers. Then there are the shafts of sunlight that do get through. Normally such shafts become visible because of the particles in the air; but here they become visible and are often so bright because they are actually shining through water, and they behave just like concentrated light beams under water. Here you may get into a little patch of direct sunlight, but the shaft or beam will vanish. Finally, on bright sunny days there is an astonishing kaleidoscopic effect if you stay still, because the sun moves so fast at the zenith that the shafts are constantly moving, or wink out as the shade of one branch or even a leaf above joins that of another branch.

Still, I saw very few animals. Several troops of monkeys came past, swinging themselves through the trees and making a great crashing, with occasional gibbers and grunts; and there were many birds, and "bugs" of all sorts, and I collected quite a number of different species of the latter. But the uproar increased for quite some time and then, very gradually, subsided.

By noon all was still, the silence only accentuated by the constant buzzings of countless insects way aloft either in the air or in the uppermost branches of the canopy. I am often asked what I mean by noise thus accentuating silence. This is almost as difficult as explaining the absolute clarity of the famous Billie Burke's remark after some terrible faux pas at a dinner party: "My dear, there was a terrible silence with things going on in it," but this is the best analogy I know. The silence of a windless northern winter night with snow on the ground is so absolute as to be leaden; in fact, how many have written that they felt sure they could "hear" it. Not only in the jungle but elsewhere throughout the tropics and especially on windless nights the silence is never glutinous like that, because of the insect noises, which are continuous and to which you become so readily adjusted or immune that you unconsciously filter them out. In the daytime, of course, the largest and rowdiest of the insects like the cicadas give out with intermittent bursts that shatter the silence, but they actually leave echoes in the jungle, while none ever stops before a hundred others roundabout have started so that even this becomes blended into the background. It's only the ones right over you that make you jump, and this, I think, because you have become attuned to the general overall uproar.

Since there was this great silence about me, what I call green silence, I took the opportunity to really look at the jungle per se. It may sound awfully trite, but I can only describe this place as an enchanted fairyland, but certainly not one such as was conjured up by European fairy tales. The great tree trunks stood rank upon rank as before, all here almost perfectly cylindrical like pillars in a cathedral but going straight up for about eighty feet before branching out, rather like gigantic starfish, with almost as giant branches. It was not till years later and in Africa while doing a botanical survey in an equivalent tract of jungle that I (and my then partners) realized that most of the giants had but four bottom branches going north-south-east-and-west, as it were. Pondering this, I became aware that the saplings that do manage to survive in this kind of forest have somehow to get up to the sunlight before they can afford to put out permanent branches. Thus they struggle upward with two pairs of the largest leaves possible, to absorb moisture and sunlight, and drop each lot as soon as the next growing tips are far enough above to take over the job. Since most trees grow on a radial arrangement, when the young sapling does reach the sunlight (directly, as it were), it puts out first one pair of permanents left and right and then, immediately, a second pair at right angles. As these develop, they provide ever more growing points, and the tree bushes out above. But how marvelously neat and orderly this process is, because all plants have to have *some* sunlight for photosynthesis, but there simply is not enough down in the cathedral of the forest, so they struggle up using but four or a few more leaves to do this and discard the lot below them without wasting material and energy in putting out woody branches.

This procedure adds greatly to the fairyland-like quality of the inner jungle because the struggling saplings stand all about so slender that you can hardly see them, but each crowned with these sort of green starfish that just seem to float in the gloom.

But there was another thing that I wondered about then and have continued increasingly to wonder at. This is that in no genuine primary jungle, i.e., one that has never been cleared and has reached its natural final form, that I have ever visited did I ever see any of the intermediate stages between the little saplings ranging in height from 6 to 50 feet and the great canopy trees. In fact, I truly begin to wonder, and as follows. (This is going to annoy a lot of people, but I strongly suggest that those who are truly interested continue to ponder this matter.) What I mean is this: Might not *four* strata in the great tiered forests represent not just stages in their continuous growth but evidence of major cataclysmic breaks? Where exactly did this endless mass of gigantic logs lying on the forest floor come from and how did they get down in there, as it were? Second, there is the main canopy of great trees interlocked with vines float-ing 80 to 150 feet up and which, judging from their trunks, must be of very great age; and then popping out of them at fairly regular intervals are what foresters call "emergents," which tower above the main canopy but with their lowest or "first" branches above the canopy. Then come the saplings, most of which would seem by their size to be of comparatively recent date—though perhaps very slow growing due to the exigencies of their struggle. Is it possible that a great forest was completely flattened except for a few supergiants (the emergents) but then, when the trouble was over, immediately sprang into life from seeds, and all went up together, forming

the canopy we see today? This would account for the
dead logs, the emergents, and the canopy. As this canopy
went up, the newer trees would have to wait ever longer
to put out their first branches. Then, when they had
embraced each other and formed a real canopy, and only
then, would the strange micro-environment for saplings
be re-created. Tree-ring dating from core borings of
tropical growth in the jungle is a tricky business if it can
actually be done, but it would be nice to know if the
present-day canopy is all of the same age. We might then
go ask the geologists if they have struck any factor that
might have so knocked down these forests in various
places and at various times; but that factor or force must
have been truly incredible, because even the worst hurricane does no more than blow a few leaves off the top of
the canopy and occasionally topple an emergent that is
rotten and dying in any case. Though here again I am
mystified, because I have yet to find an emergent that is
rotten or hollow as so many of the bigger trees in the
canopy are.

Which brings me to the next thing that I pondered that
morning.

Sitting on one of these great, moss-grown logs and
seeing that there was obviously no place for them to have
grown, it was brought most forcibly to my mind that I
was looking at this world upon altogether a wrong time
scale. Indeed, I knew that some trees grow to an immense individual age, from our point of view, in many
parts of the world, and that wood may last seemingly
forever in certain climates and conditions, but any seri-
ous-minded idiot could see here that this constituted an
anomaly. Growth per se proceeds at a terrifying rate in

the tropics, but only up to a point (the canopy level of that area); then it seems virtually to stop. Just how fast could this canopy form such a roof over its fallen parents? And tropical foresters have often stated that they suspect some of the so-called primary-jungle forest of being just very old *secondary* forest. In other words, they are saying that there was once a mass clearance. However, this was most certainly not done by man, so we have to take a deep breath and be prepared to admit that such clearings were truly geological on the time scale. Which brings me right back to what I was saying before.

Thus I was forced on that my first morning in "the jungle" to begin philosophizing. It was all so different from that which I had been brought up to and taught. It was my first real confrontation with "You can't have it both ways."

The "jungle," as envisioned by practically everybody who has not been there, did exist on this estate, since this tangled growth—the result of plentiful sunlight—is found at the outermost edge of the primary forest, in areas that have been cleared and then allowed to revert to their natural state, along rivers and such. It was here that I did most of my actual collecting on this first lap of my trip. My host supplied a small boy to act as bearer or *chokera*, and another visitor—a very good-looking young Scot—who was a keen bug hunter like myself, and I went out on several occasions, draped round with bottles, nets, guns, and everything else we thought might be useful. I later learned better methods, but we did bring down a beautiful squirrel and a bat, which promptly bit me badly on the finger and necessitated our returning to the main house to dress it. Undeterred, we set out again for a small patch of jungle where monkeys were found and shot a hugely fat female that came crashing to the ground at the second shot. This we carried back in triumph and then set out still again for another place where we filled my bottles with several good things besides about thirty species of dragonfly of every color imaginable.

I rose at a reasonable hour the next morning and proceeded to clean the monkey's skin, since I had to leave the next day. Needless to say, the helpful house boys brought me several lizards and bugs, and I became so snowed under with work, and the ants became so numerous, and the smell so bad, that I nearly gave up "bug hunting." After lunch I continued to prepare and pack both my specimens and my clothes and equipment when my Scots friend turned up with a lot of bugs, another squirrel, and a seven-foot water snake! He must have sensed my desperation, for, like the gentleman he was, he pitched in, and together we somehow got everything shipshape for my departure early the next morning.

The drive this time was slow as it was a public holiday and every native was out in his very gaudiest and best; also, Mr. Chung Junior was not at the wheel. I reached the ferry in good time and was transported back to Pinang where I boarded a local vessel to make the trip to Sumatra.

❧ 5 ❧

My Introduction to Sumatra; and a Slight
Oversight—A Tiger

A S WE NEARED BELAWAN,
the port for Medan, but while still some miles at sea, we
had to pass through a kind of maze made of fishing traps
—rings of posts stuck into the sea bottom—which
seemed to go on indefinitely. However, we wended our
way through, and then, through the expertise (or just
plain "pull") of a charming Hollander who had been sent
to meet me and get me on the road for Medan, I waltzed
through Customs without having my bags examined or
my passport inspected. My letter from the British Museum also helped. I soon got off in a car provided by an
old friend of my mother's, to whom I had wired the date
of my arrival. The drive to Medan in the cool of the
morning took about thirty-five minutes. The people were
pure Malayans here, the young men very good-looking,

small, gay, and not at all cheeky; the women dressed in gay sarongs and tight-fitting blouses with silk shawls over their heads. The country at first was quite open, but nearer Medan palm jungle begins and there were numerous little wooden houses. I was safely deposited at my host's bungalow where I was immediately made to feel at home. And my host at once set about making arrangements for me to stay at a tobacco plantation up in the hills. This took several days and was not, as it proved, quite what I had expected.

In the meantime, I happily collected bugs in an overgrown garden next door and was passed from hand to hand by all the local zoologists, who could not have been more helpful and charming. They showed me through their various small museums, and even took the trouble to drive me to likely spots where I might find specimens I was specifically looking for. On one occasion we stopped at a native house to get water for the car. Attached to the house was a little thatched structure in which paddy [rice in the straw] was stored; on top of the pile of paddy was a mat with a plate of food and some lemon squash, which the owner explained was for the spooks, to satisfy their appetite and so keep them away from the paddy. On the way home we were brought several mice and rats and at one stop returned to our car to find two young mousangs or Palm-Civets (*Paradoxurus*) offered for sale. These are rather nondescript little animals, mousy gray-brown, with a dark face, limbs, and tail, but always with light markings under the eyes. They are found all the way from the southern slopes of the Himalayas through Malaya to Java. There are several species, but all can be classed as pests. They attack poultry and raid kitchens but are perhaps most awful at night when they delight in romping about on the "pan" roofs so common in Indonesia. They keep up this racket for hours, particularly on moonless nights, and make sleep utterly impossible. I should have liked to have had them —as specimens—but their owner wanted five guilders each, which was far too much.

I also acquired a bamboo-rat, a gift from the head zoologist at the local museum, who had his private Malay taxidermist preserve it for me. When I went to collect this, I was informed that The Arrangements were complete and I must leave almost at once! Unbeknownst to me, he had been helping my host in this regard, and they meant business. I packed furiously with the help of a house boy, and soon a fine Buick turned up with the little man who was to be my driver. He was a very perfect little Malay, about twenty, very good-looking, clean (his nails and hands spotless), and enthusiastic. He brought with him a very fine little suitcase and a large jar of arsenical soap!

We drove furiously for about an hour, mostly through cultivated country, in a westerly direction toward Berastagi. We passed two little towns, one of which was teeming with people, a football match and a wedding being in progress. The latter was a procession with a hundred or so banners made of gay-colored flowers. We made a wrong turn once but circled around one of the ubiquitous rice fields and hurtled back onto our road, now heading northwest from Medan, skirting grazing buffalo, rocking between scurries of golden-brown children and scattering the feathered world in cackling flight. The back of the driver's neck perspired and glistened against a backdrop of distant heliotrope mountains.

At lunchtime we swooped across a long wooden bridge and came to a halt before a beautiful white house with flanking bougainvillea-loaded pergolas amid the ringing calls of captive parrots. My bags were unloaded, a moderate heap of shiny guilders was handed over, and I entered the cool porch, my driver turning around to go back to Medan—complete with his jar of arsenical soap. A tall, portly blond man advanced from the shadows with outstretched hand.

"Ah, I expect you. Yes?" he said, bowing gravely.

We went through the house and out onto an immaculate lawn where a table groaning with fruit was laid for lunch. The beautiful garden was banked with strange tropical flowers, and large, leaf-filled wire cages or pens surrounded it upon all sides.

"So you will go to Lau Boentoe?" my host enquired, and when I had confirmed his surmise, he looked interested.

"You are lucky," he said, "if you like the animals. I do not go myself, but that part has many fine birds. People do not know it well."

For the rest of lunch we continued much in the same vein, for our interests were identical and we had much to say. We then inspected the cages.

"Here you will find," said my host with a wave of his large pink hand, "almost all the animals of this country. Before, I was having many more, but now I concentrate to make my living collection complete."

And it was complete. Although I had composed a list

of the fauna reported from Sumatra, there were many here that I had never seen before. There were monkeys and civet cats and birds and rats and lizards and snakes. This man's garden was not a menagerie; it was a concentrated pocket of the wildlife of the island. For two hours this immaculate giant of a man in his starched white suit walked among his captive flock smoking an enormous cheroot. The shyest of animals came and stood by him while he talked. He tickled the most aggressive behind their woolly ears with his big manicured but tobacco-stained forefinger. All sat quietly staring away from us while the hair on their backs rose and fell at his touch. He also had six dogs and a very tame Orang-Utan named Pete, and the latter joined us on the verandah and drank beer after my tour was completed.

As the fires of the tropical sun wilted away and the afternoon haze shimmered golden, a horrible noise approached the house. My host produced a huge watch from his breast and surveying its face said, "Ah. The Englishman," and led the way to the front of the house. We emerged onto the road just in time to see a great screw of dust swerve sideways into a gap in the hedge. Before the dust had slowed down, moreover, there was an agonized crashing of cheap metal, and something shot backward out into the road. More dust charged forward, enveloping the tormented apparition; there was a further uproar, and a car shot out of the cloud and came to a rocking halt before us.

Six natives leaped out as if shot from a pigeon gun, disclosing a small, very tanned man waving a huge briar pipe. My host, chuckling enormously, introduced me. He was obviously very pleased. He beamed upon the man in

the car, who was glaring at me. "Oh!" said the latter, still
staring fixedly at me. He paused and then fairly bellowed
at me, "Well, get in, get in if you want to come. The
road's awful. Boy!" he yelled, "Bring those bags, hurry
up!" And all the time he kept revving the palsied engine
so that acrid blue fumes belched from all sides, mingling
with the dust. "Hurry up!" he yelled at his hurrying
minions and, still glaring, added as an afterthought, in
my direction, "How d'ye do, or something, er."

I climbed into the car, and before I had had time to
sufficiently thank my host for his hospitality, a pile of
chattering natives tumbled in almost on top of me and
the car leaped forward. The preliminary leap was followed by a succession of irregular bounds which quickly
flattened out into a headlong rush that didn't slacken for
half an hour. We traveled in silence as far as conversation
was concerned, but the general noise was terrific. We
dived through fords, we crashed through piles of dead
branches, and every time one of the hapless natives who
were flying about the interior of the after-portion of the
car like shot in a rattle opened his mouth, my strange
new companion removed the pipe from his mouth and
bawled, "Shut up!" The rest of the time he gripped the
wheel and the muscles stood out over his jaw bone.

The road, as my new host had succinctly observed, was
bad. In fact, to my uninitiated eyes it did not exist over
long stretches. After two hours we began mounting a
very steep hill by what appeared to be the bed of a river.
As the soft night closed on us we roared over a grassy
slope and performed those excruciating gyrations that
had immediately preceded this person's arrival at the
house of the Hollander below. We stopped before a ram-

bling house and, aching and shaking and constantly exhorted in a loud voice from behind, I jumped out of the car.

The view that met my sweeping gaze could not possibly have been surpassed. Bank upon bank of gently rising hills bathed in mauve mist cut by shafts of golden light unfolded in all directions. The hill upon which this house stood was composed of bright-red earth marbled with emerald-green turf. It was surrounded by a great natural moat, at the bottom of which wound a bright-blue river. Beyond it rose a battlement of puffy, bluish-green verdure, like a giant quilt caught in by giant stitches here and there. Over the lip of this encircling battlement to the southeast stretched the flat coastal plain like a child's map. I was hustled onto the wide verandah of the house.

My host disappeared within, to the accompaniment of prolonged bellows and the pattering of quite an army of bare feet. Orders rang out from unexpected quarters of the house for half an hour, while I waited smoking and watching the fall of night. I was startled by a crash and the marching of heavy boots. I looked around, startled; my host had appeared in a clean khaki shirt, riding breeches, and superbly cut riding boots.

"Not had a bath yet?" he shouted and, seeing me wince a bit, added not unkindly, "Must have a bath, you know."

I retired to hurry through my ablutions as a booming temple gong rent the silence.

Dinner, served upon a highly polished table of local wood, was excellent. Five servants were kept busy serving, and the whole business was disposed of in less time than it takes to down the soup in normal households. I ventured a few remarks out of deference to my position as guest in the household, but was not encouraged. My host invariably answered in monosyllables. After this meal, over which I would have liked to linger, we went charging out to the verandah and swallowed a cup of boiling coffee.

"Ah," said my host, long before I had finished. "Ride?"

I was so taken aback by the question that I could only splutter a bit. I remember to this day wondering dimly what I should ride; visions of a childhood donkey flashed before me. Like a drowning man clutching at a straw, I came up with the incautious reply that I did a bit.

"Always ride after dinner. No time in the morning. Boy! Boy! Where is the damned fellow?" and he was gone through the house.

A few minutes later we set out. The moon was just rising; I clung to the largest bunch of my mount's mane that I could gather into my hand under cover of darkness and was relieved to find that we descended the steep hill very gently.

"Show you around a bit," said my host.

Thinking this took the form of a question, I answered brightly that I should be grateful, though it was as dark as the proverbial dungeon at the bottom of the valley.

"See it now or never," I was told. "No time in the day."

And "see" it I did, seedling beds, coolie lines, water tanks, the beginnings of paths leading to half a dozen villages with names that meant nothing to me, and finally, the first fully grown tobacco field laid out by this estate [see Figure 11, Lau Boentoe Estate].

"No good," said my host. "Too hilly for tobacco."
Then he explained further, "Grow the young plants up
here better than on the plain."

We rode on.

The path we now took entered a great black arch in the
side of the forest. It was pitch dark within and the horses
picked their way cautiously. After some minutes we came
out into bright moonlight at the base of a deep gorge.
The trail rose gradually up the right-hand bank of this,
passing through arbors of inky blackness, under giant
fleurs-de-lis of bamboo and across alternating open
areas carpeted with ground mimosa, above which nothing else will grow. It was a perfect equatorial night filled
with the whirring of crickets and rent by the occasional
howls of big-eyed night birds.

My host relaxed a bit. He became quite communica-
tive. I asked him about the animals of the district and
gained the impression that he considered all naturalists,
scientists, and other bug hunters a single species of a
very low form of animal life. In reply to my query as to
what animals I might be able to obtain by shooting, he
observed:

"You saw 'em all at lunch on the way up. That fellow
knows more about it than I do. Collected all his life.
Never carry a gun myself." We rode on.

"Take you back by the next gorge," he suddenly announced as we veered to the right. "Good place for your
damned bug hunting, I should think. Better see it."

As we emerged from this second gorge, at the foot of
the hill upon which the bungalow stood, he drew my
attention to the path that led to it. I considered this
thoughtful of him, for the topography of the place was

most muddling. We ascended to the house and, after a brief talk and a drink, retired to bed.

For three weeks I busied myself with my work, collecting all the local fauna I could unearth. It was varied and plentiful, and I found that the gorge through which we had returned to the house on the first night was indeed the best location, just as my host had indicated. That gentleman did not accompany me again, as I was very busy at night with the day's catches and he was fully occupied throughout the day. At the crack of dawn his voice would ring out from the mists at the bottom of the little valley surrounding the house. At eight o'clock we breakfasted for a second time, and immediately afterward he would take a small saddlebag and rush out of the house again, never to reappear before the difficult hour of two-thirty when lunch was served.

I was always out during the afternoon, but whatever time I got back, my host never appeared from his room until five-thirty.

Rather late one afternoon I set out once more for the gorge where most of my collecting had been done. I carried a butterfly net, for I was after insects. Ascending the path up the almost perpendicular side of the gorge, I was lost in contemplation.

All of a sudden a crashing ahead brought me up sharp. The bank was covered with giant bamboos that grew in semicircular clumps. Behind these, the huge dead leaves of wild teak trees gathered to a great depth. They were dry and crackled like parchment when anything stirred within them. I saw that something was moving within one such embattlement and advanced toward it. A large monitor lizard appeared.

Wanting another of these for my collection, I decided to chance an unlikely capture with the butterfly net and so left the path and advanced cautiously. Just as I was ready to pop the net over the creature's wildly staring and immobile face, there was an explosion and, amid a cloud of dead leaves, the animal projected itself out over the slope. I made a last desperate swipe, missed, lost my balance, and instantly followed the flying animal headlong down the steep incline. The ground was of wet clay and there was no stopping. I descended at considerable speed and arrived at the narrow bottom of the gulley in a sitting posture, though still clutching the butterfly net.

Somewhat rattled, I began to pick myself up. In doing so I happened to glance across to the opposite bank not a dozen yards away, where there was an open patch covered in mimosa. My legs gave way, and I gently subsided again, for right before me, ankle-deep in the mimosa, its whiskered face turned full upon me over its shoulder, stood a small but immensely muscled tiger.

For many seconds—they only seemed like hours—it surveyed me with its glittering eyes, meticulously inspecting my person, the butterfly net that I still held aloft and, finally, myself again. Then it opened its black-lipped mouth, gave a low hissing sound, yawned, glanced at me once more, and stalked off into the bushes beyond.

For a long time I just continued to sit, giggling from time to time, doing nothing constructive and in a complete daze. It was the first time I had seen one of the great cats on the same side of the bars as myself and, what was much worse, there had been a slight oversight on my part. I quite frankly had no idea that tigers were found in Sumatra. Somehow I had just never considered the question of the detailed distribution of the tiger and had missed it in compiling my list of the animals of the country. Of course, I was after *small* mammals, and neither my Dutch friend with his zoo representing the "complete" fauna of the island nor my host had ever mentioned the animal, though we had talked of every other imaginable form of life. I could not then speak the language of the natives, and I hadn't seen the skins of any tigers since my arrival. However, the more I thought of the matter, sitting there on the clay bank, the more vividly I began to remember passages in one book after another that referred to the tigers of the islands; also everything I had ever heard about man-eating tigers, including the tigress that had been killed by the famous Jim Corbett not too many years before [presumably the Champawat maneater, a tigress that killed a known total of 438 people in eight years, killed by Corbett in 1911].

When I had overcome my first fright and my much greater general astonishment, I gathered up my scattered possessions and passed out of the gorge in a manner and at a speed devoid of all dignity. As I gained the house, panting wildly, my host emerged from his room, all starch and polish. It was just five-thirty.

"Get anything?" he asked, a question that had become almost a formula at our afternoon meetings.

Between gasps I announced that I had seen a tiger!

"Tiger, tiger?" he said. "Where?"

"In the second gorge."

"Not surprised," he said as he reached for the decanter. "Lives there, you know. Got cubs under the fourth big bamboo clump."

I was frozen to the edge of the verandah; a wild galaxy of questions, thoughts, recollections of myself groveling all over that gorge, poking into holes after insects and snails whirled through my mind. Finally, all these came to rest like homing pigeons on a memory of our ride on the night of my arrival and of my host's remarks on the subject of shooting. I attempted more conversation on the subject to relieve my feelings but I was reminded that my bath awaited me. Then the rush of dinner came on and immediately afterward my host went to bed.

Two days later I left for the coast. My host bade me a warm good-bye.

"Glad to have put you up, hope you can drop in later on," were his parting remarks as he leaped away in his tin chariot from the door of the large Hollander's house.

"Well?" said my friend the Hollander, "And the animals, you find them much?"

"Yes" I answered rather mechanically.

"The Englishman, he helps you?"

"Indeed, he was very kind and helpful."

"You are shown the big gorge and collect many butterflies?"

"Yes," I answered, "But do you know . . . ?"

He waved my remarks aside. "Perhaps because you are an Englishman, too, he show you that place at once. He never invite me yet."

"Really? And why not?"

The big man looked at me long and earnestly. "Because," he said, "he is the greatest collector of butterflies in this whole part of the world."

"What! You mean to say he is himself a bug hunter? But he seems to loathe all collectors."

"He pretends to despise everything, but he is only joking."

"Listen, Mijnheer, do you call it joking to show me a valley at night without a gun, tell me it was the best place for insects, and then let me go there every day unarmed when he knew a tiger had cubs there?"

"Gott!" the Hollander exploded. "I forget the tiger; yes, he always do that. He thinks it a very big joke! He goes there himself every day to study the breeding of the butterflies."

Though one may grumble somewhat at the Englishman's sense of humor, it is true that in fact I was not in any real danger. Unless a tiger has turned man-eater, always because of physical disability of some kind,* it simply ignores people, *vide* Corbett's story of a small boy, probably himself, stalking jungle fowl, only to have a tiger appear on the other side of "his" bush; the tiger turned around and looked at the boy "with an expression on its face which said as clearly as any words, 'Hello, kid, what the hell are you doing here?' and, receiving no answer," turned around and walked away without a backward look. But I did not know all this at the time.

---

*With the possible exception of cubs raised by a man-eater, a question never satisfactorily answered. [S. W. S.]

6

Achi and the Metallic Green Beetles: A Lesson in Hospitality

I HAD BEEN STAYING IN THE homes of hospitable Dutch folk and had acquired a "servant" through the kindness of a Dutchman holding an official position. This lad, Achi, was in many ways exceptional, though this had perhaps been obscured for two reasons. He was the first Malay servant I had ever had, so that I lacked experience for comparison and, secondly, although working for a wage, his work was by no means menial. His position was, in fact, that of interpreter, courier, and technical assistant, in addition to the business of skinning and preparing animals for which I had hired him and for which he had received some training during the course of employment at a government agricultural establishment. I had been further misled by the fact that, although appearing rather well educated and distinctly cultured, he had adhered to native costume with jacket, sarong, and small velvet fez, whereas most educated natives soon adopted European clothes.

Achi was, in fact, invaluable, as you will learn.

There is, in the mountainous area southwest of Medan, a group of people called the Achinese, a very proud folk. For one historical reason and another, none relevant to this narrative, these people did not hold their technical rulers—the Hollanders—in very high esteem, and when I landed in Sumatra there was a persistent rumor current to the effect that the last eight Hollanders who had entered Achin (or Atjeh) had remained there forever in a sadly dissected condition. I was never able to determine the truth or the particulars of this story, but I did learn that its corollary was that the Achinese were very friendly toward the English, reputedly because of an ancient trade treaty between the two peoples. It was therefore with something akin to shock that I discovered that Achi was an Achinese.

How came it that he was outside Achinese territory, I enquired, and was surprised to hear that there were many Achinese in the rest of Sumatra. They came to learn Hollands, my servant informed me, and he, together with most of his countrymen, passed themselves off as Javanese or other Malay nationalities from other islands.

The day after learning all this I watched Achi for a long time while we worked opposite each other at a small table in an outhouse of the estate where we were staying. I was greatly impressed by his quiet efficiency. That evening I was very forcibly struck by something else.

I came upon him unexpectedly amongst the shrub-
bery. He was bowed double toward Mecca on a tastefully
colored prayer mat. After much deliberation, some enquiries among the estate management, and further observation of the fellow, I gently brought a conversation
around to the subject of the mountainous land of Achin.
I expected a certain frigidity but I was greatly mistaken.

No sooner had I raised the subject than I was subjected
to a long and penetrating political exposition and, before
I had time to recover, I was given a detailed account of
the geography of Achin, with pencil sketches on the tablecloth for my especial edification; this was followed by
a most intelligent discourse upon the customs and daily
life of the country people. Rather taken aback by this
outburst—in quite good English withal—I asked several
leading questions and was duly enlightened.

"Why do you tell me all this?" I finally asked, adding,
"I have heard that you don't like the Dutch."

"Because, Tuan," he replied instantly, "You are English and not an *Orang Blunda*," meaning that I was an
English Tuan and not a Dutchman.

The significance of the word "tuan" as opposed to
"orang" was not lost on me when I came to consider the
Orang-Utan or "Wild Man." Feeling rather awkward
about the position thus created for our cousin nation the
Dutch, for whom I personally have the greatest respect
and liking, I let the matter drop for the time.

Some days later we moved farther north and camped
near a small village in the jungle. When we had established ourselves and mounted a hill to view the surrounding country, my remarkable servant became very

quiet. Then, as we stood on the summit, he pointed away to the north and said simply, "There, Tuan, is my home. I do not see my father for very long, and he is old."

Sensing the true significance of this remark, I evinced interest in the country away by the mountains but otherwise held my own council. Three days later it came out. I was asked whether I would care to visit his country and had my answer ready. I said that I would, as I relied upon my guide to explain fully to his compatriots that not only was I not a Hollander but that, in any case, I came only with friendship and interest in my heart. When, therefore, our work in this place was finished, we set about making preparations for our trip, and the first difficulty immediately became apparent.

Nobody from the village near which we lived or from any other nearby village—all of which were inhabited by Hill Batuks—would even consider carrying our possessions into Achinese country. Suspecting the nationality of my servant, they gave no specific reasons but produced a large assortment of excuses. After prolonged debate, therefore, we decided to travel exceedingly light, carrying all that we needed ourselves. I was induced to do this by Achi, who was most enthusiastic about the whole enterprise and assured me that I should want for nothing as soon as we reached his home. The insistence of the lad upon this point made me speculate on the nature of his family "surroundings." Even the Hill Batuks lived better than the average European town worker, and I had no doubt that I should not lack food.

Our decision, moreover, automatically settled several other problems for us, since no carriers meant no extra food supplies, no need for fresh supplies of cash, and no difficult arrangements for extracting ourselves later on. It would mean a considerable curtailment of my normal schedule of work because of lack of equipment; but then, I had come to look upon the whole trip as a kind of holiday.

I entertained some qualms on the day of our departure, for only then did I learn that there was no path leading to our destination. I had no experience then of the facility with which one may get lost in tropical forests, otherwise I would never have been persuaded to set out. Nevertheless, I viewed the proposition of a couple of nights in the jungle under a small mosquito net with some misgivings. I also wondered dimly whether the Achinese were quite clear in their minds about the difference between the Hollanders and the English. One white man is normally considered as bad as another in the East.

However, we left early one morning, sped on our way by an assortment of silent, wide-eyed stares from the village through which we had to pass. We entered the jungle at the bottom of a tremendous valley that stretched away to the distant blue peaks, around which the lightning played every evening and which always seemed so remote. We carried, in addition to the mosquito net, my treasured shotgun and fifty cartridges, several tins of sardines, a canvas bag full of biscuits, salt, two pots of marmalade, and other items of food; two small saucepans that fitted into one another, skinning instruments and a roll of cotton wool, two insect cases with pins and other small items for the preparation of insects, two blankets and a small groundsheet of light canvas, some clothes, a few simple medicaments, and an assortment of other small essentials chosen by Achi. The total came to about seventy pounds, of which I carried about twenty-five to thirty, and this only under protest from my eager guide and after I had pointed out that we would thus travel quicker.

During the whole of the first day we toiled up the bed of a boulder-strewn river in the cool shade of the forest. We stopped for two small meals and finally made our humble camp on a clear bank at the intersection of two tributaries. A palm shelter was erected for my comfort and dinner prepared. Had I been carrying evening clothes they would doubtless have been neatly laid out for me on the groundsheet. At sundown we went hunting and came upon a family party of tapirs (*Tapirus indicus*) sleeping in the stream bed.

The great lumbering black-and-white beasts were as truly camouflaged among the boulders as the textbooks would have us believe. Later we shot a large, screaming bird for our pot and collected some butterflies that I hoped would be valuable. The night was dry and warm, and I felt very satisfied with life. The following day was a continuation of this almost idyllic existence, though I noticed a perceptible change coming over my companion.

No longer could this person be referred to as a servant of any form. He was slowly adopting a protective rather than a patronizing air and, though the high-sounding title of Tuan was scrupulously adhered to, I found myself a pupil of the art of bushcraft. I was well satisfied by this state of affairs since I recognized my incompetence in this respect.

About midday, we emerged from the top of the valley upon a small plateau covered with tall, waving grass. We turned sharply to the right and came out upon a further small, level, grassy area that jutted out from the side of the mountains like a box at a theatre. Here we paused.

"I bring you here to show you where it changes," my guide said. He then indicated the direction from which we had come. "There is the Colony," and then, turning to the left, he added proudly, "and here is my country. Come, we go."

We descended a steep valley veering to the left, mounted a high ridge, and then descended another steep valley. At the bottom of this we came upon quite a large river splashing among great rocks. By it we made our camp, but the evening was not quite so idyllic. It rained with considerable fury, as is customary among tropical mountains. We slept little and got very wet and cold, for the groundsheet had to be used to protect our belongings.

The next evening we came out upon a tiny trail and, following this, we arrived after dark at a large village. Here I was left in the shadows at the end of the "street" between the huge, pent-roof houses while my guide went ahead, telling me that I might expect to be left for some time. Finally he returned, accompanied by half a dozen young men who bowed formally to me, picked up my belongings, and set off down the "street."

"How do you find your father?" I asked.

My young friend beamed, "He is well, Tuan; he welcomes you. It is long since foreigners visited him, and he has much to tell you. My father," he added, "is a hadji."

I came to an abrupt halt, for this was news to me indeed. A hadji is one who has made a pilgrimage to Mecca and, in Malaya, is usually not only a man of importance but one of substance, at least proportionately to his home community. This was the first time I had heard of my companion's position.

We eventually came to a very beautiful house built in the native style but of much greater grandeur. Surprisingly enough, it was surrounded by a garden. Around it were congregated many people: very clean, upstanding, dignified people. We ascended a steep flight of steps, for the house stood upon piles. On the verandah above stood a most majestic old gentleman in national costume with the white turban of the hadji. He welcomed me warmly in halting English and, taking my proffered hand, led me into the house.

That house was intriguing in its beauty and unusualness. Its high roof was supported upon blackened wood rafters, its furniture was also of dark wood with a subdued polish. It was filled with brasswork and batik covers. It was quite unlike a European house and equally unlike the houses of either Europeanized natives of the country or well-to-do peasants. It resembled more one's conception—doubtless erroneous—of a sultan's palace, though in miniature. This, moreover, was precisely what it was, though my host was in no way a sultan.

He was head of the village, though exactly what percentage of his authority was temporal and what spiritual, I never fully comprehended. For myself, the most outstanding aspect of this quietly imposing gentleman was his erudition, his humor, his graceful manners and the other facets that composed his almost regal demeanor.

The days that I spent under his roof were among the most delightful that I have ever spent away from my own home. During that period, I learned more of the true values of human life and of civilization—or rather, the antithesis of it as we know it—than I had ever learned previously or have ever done since. For many hours and despite the difficulties of language, we conversed upon all manner of topics. I was also introduced to the teachings of the Koran and, perhaps fortunately, discovered a profound interest in these holy profundities of Islam.

At the same time, I carried on my work at great speed, for all the younger generation were instructed by my host to render assistance, which they did with a will and despite their obvious amusement at my odd interests. As a result, my meagre supplies were soon exhausted. I pointed this out to Achi, who discussed the matter with his father. The latter pressed me to stay, and in the end I acquiesced, though Achi insisted upon performing his role as my employee by making the journey back to our base to collect fresh supplies. He had been gone four days when I made my mistake.

I had gone out as usual in search of animals, accompanied by two of the keenest small boys in the village. As I was returning, I came upon a large fallen tree by the path and began stripping the bark from its trunk. Under this I found a number of large beetles entirely clad in an armor of brilliant, shimmering, metallic peacock green. They were so beautiful, so much larger than any other green beetles that I had found in the country, and so obviously of a totally different kind, that I bottled them eagerly. The two boys watched me in silence. Then they ran ahead to the village.

When I reached my host's house I encountered a large crowd. They made way for me but did not return my evening greetings and remained silent and sensibly hostile. I felt uneasy and went in search of my host. One of the women, however, expressed by signs that he was busy in a closed part of the house and, considerably mystified, I retired to deal with my catches. This I did upon a verandah in view of the crowd below. After a time I began to feel very nervous but continued my work. It was not until near sundown that my host appeared and addressed the crowd with some vigor. After this they departed and, waiting till they had all gone, the old man finally turned to me.

With great precision in the mixture of English and such kitchen Malay as I knew, he gave me to understand that I must give him all my collections and bottles and that I must not leave his house. In explanation he would say nothing. His tone was not unkindly, but it was very firm, and I handed over my treasures. The following day I spent under "house arrest," holding communion with no one. Having no books, I was bored and fretful; besides, I was rapidly becoming rather alarmed, for the more I thought about it, the more unpleasant my position appeared. My guide had left me, I did not know exactly where I was, I was a foreigner in a country where by all accounts foreigners are not welcome, and nobody knew of my whereabouts. Then, quite by chance, I came upon a large leather-bound edition of the Koran beautifully illuminated. Although I knew nothing of Arabic in which it was written, I sat down on the rug and, opening the book, began to glance through the pages.

While I was thus engaged, one of the women chanced along the verandah. Seeing me, she bolted into the house and, imagining that I had again offended, I was about to get up when my host came running out. He sat down before me and, taking one of my hands in his own, began to talk earnestly. This is the gist of what he said as far as I could make out:

His people, although professing to be devout Mo-hammedans, retained a multiplicity of earlier fetishistic beliefs, the strongest of which concerned the metallic green beetles, which were held in special reverence by them. He himself held no such beliefs, but what temporal authority he had was founded upon his spiritual ascend-ancy based on his position as a devout Mohammedan and a hadji. They now held him personally responsible for my actions since I was staying in his house. Now, however, he found me absorbed in the Koran and felt that it might be possible that in reality I was a follower of the Prophet and not, as had been popularly supposed, an infidel. If this was so, he would be able to explain to the villagers that I undoubtedly only tampered with the beetles out of temporary curiosity and with no malicious intent nor even through lack of proper guidance on his part since I was a Mohammedan and not an infidel and therefore unable to do serious wrong.

I had to consider very quickly. As far as I could see, there was but one way out of the quandary, so I sailed as near a compromise as possible by stating that I was not a practicing Christian (in fact, I wasn't) and that I bore the principles of Islam in the highest esteem, but that I realized myself but an elementary student of the words of the Prophet (true, too!). This apparently sufficed for the hadji. He rose forthwith and addressed the men of the village. The parley was protracted but the results satisfactory. I could not collect insects nor leave the village until his son returned; but, then, I had no intention at that point of doing either.

Achi at last arrived the next evening, having been held up by local flooding of the riverbed we had used as a trail, and greeted me warmly—as did the other men who had come with him. It appeared that I had been forgiven, for we were allowed to collect insects again, and after a few days, my cases were again full and we made our departure. I was genuinely sorry to leave, despite the unfortunate interlude.

Our journey back followed the same route. When we came to the high grass plateau, it was evening and we decided to camp there for the night. After the meal had been eaten, Achi turned to me and spoke. This is roughly what he said:

"Tuan, we are leaving my country. I am sad, but I am also very happy, because I feared at one time that you might think me a bad friend and a bad servant and a bad man. Had it not been for good fortune and the fact that you were a friend of my father and interested in the Holy Book and that my father is a very wise man, unfortunate things might have happened to you. By shutting those beetles up in a bottle you greatly frightened the common people of my country, for they find them very holy, not being true followers of the Prophet. They demanded to be allowed to remove you, but my father protected you by guaranteeing that you remain in his house. Later he was able to show all men that you were studying the Koran and assured them that you were indeed not an infidel. Still they were not satisfied nor trusting and demanded that you still be kept until my return. They came to question me about you while I was still far away from the village."

"But what did you say?" I asked in retrospective consternation. "Surely you did not tell them that I was a hadji or something."

"No, Tuan, I did not, but I told them that I had worked with you for many months and that I could promise that you were not a Christian Infidel, for you see, my father did not believe you either and so sent my mother secretly to meet me on the road. She told me what had happened and what my father instructed me to say."

"But you were all taking great risks for me," I said.

"You were my father's guest, and we were responsible for your well-being," he replied simply, adding, "One thing I pray of you, Tuan, that is not to enter a church of the Christians before you leave Sumatra, for there are many of my people, and if it became known, I would never dare to return to my country."

I gladly gave him the requested assurance—a small price for such magnificent hospitality. Achi traveled with me throughout the islands and, although he adhered to the outward forms of master and servant, he was truly a friend and probably the best teacher I ever had.

7

Gibbons; How to Climb a Tree; Flying Lizards; Smelly Ones; Mangrove Swamps and Mud-skippers

---

To me the most magnificent animal to be found in Sumatra is the Siamang *(Symphalangus syndactylus)*, one of the Lesser Apes and related to the Gibbons and Concolors. It has rather long, thick, somewhat shaggy jet-black fur but a naked face, with sparse stubble for a mustache and beard. The arms are extremely long, and the hair on the forearm grows toward the elbow just as it does in the Great Apes and on us, thus providing a "drip tip" for rainy days. Both the males and the females have large sacs under the chin that can be inflated from the throat and help to produce the astonishing vocalizations of the Siamang.

The Siamangs, unlike the Wow-Wows or Silvery Gibbons *(Hylobates moloch)*, are almost never kept as pets by the Indonesians, since they generally run away if left unchained and also have a rather odd temperament. As they grow older they become very surly and sometimes truly vicious. Inasmuch as large males may weigh as much as forty-five pounds and stand a bit over three feet tall, they can be more than a handful and in fact frightfully dangerous. But in their native haunts they are magnificent. Their home is the upper canopy of the forest and they do not often come to the ground, though they are actually more truly bipedal than the Great Apes (Orang-Utans or *Mias,* Chimps, and Gorillas). At dawn and at sundown they make the mountain valleys literally ring with their tremendous, prolonged, barking hoots that, led off by one and taken up by all others within hearing, mount to a deafening crescendo that makes your eardrums ring and reduces every other jungle creature, even the most raucous birds, to abject silence. This uproar usually stops abruptly, and then echoes go rolling away over the canyons until other, distant troupes pick up the call. Then off they all go again. When disturbed, or sometimes apparently just to amuse themselves, they literally roar through the trees, running along branches on their hind legs with a sort of loping gallop, waving their arms and howling, and when they come to the end of a branch they just sail out into space to seize a branch with the ease of an expert acrobat, and then go swinging along hand over hand in great swoops, covering up to twenty feet between the point of release with one hand and the seizure of another branch with the next. In full flight, moreover, they are actually airborne longer than they are attached to the trees. Even at "low speed" they normally run along horizontal branches, holding their long arms above their heads or at other strange angles

—both as balancing organs and merely to get them out of the way—until the branch becomes so slim that they have once again to brachiate.

Perhaps it was watching these magnificent creatures in the high forests of Sumatra that finally led me to decide to get up into the canopy, though the notion had been in my mind for some time. There seemed to be so much going on up there! You cannot, however, simply climb a tree in the jungle. There are no low branches, and I was not provided with mountaineering gear. So, as usual, I consulted Achi, who said, more or less, "I fix."

Achi's first step was to make a primitive bow and arrow; these bore little resemblance to the armaments sold by "purveyors" to great white hunters but proved to be most efficient. He then unraveled a very long thread from an old piece of cloth and tied one end of this to the arrow, giving the free end to me to hold. Then came the hard part. There were plenty of branches, but none was conveniently situated away from other branches, vines, and general canopy debris, so Achi simply shot his arrow up into the canopy and hoped. This went on for some time, the arrow always being retrieved with great care so as not to break the to us infinitely valuable thread; but Achi persisted and was finally rewarded when the arrow came down over a branch and landed neatly, carrying the thread with it. Putting the arrow aside, Achi tied our lightest fishing line to the thread and hauled it aloft and over the branch. When this was safely done, he tied a strong strand of liana to the fishing line and hauled this up and over. Then, making a loop in the liana to provide a simple sling, he climbed aboard and announced that I should haul him up to the lowest branch. Fortunately, he was considerably lighter than I and could also help by hauling on the downcoming portion of the liana, and thus we got him up. After that I managed to get up on a maze of lianas hauled aloft to serve almost as a ladder, and we scrambled toward the top of the tree. Suddenly the whole world looked different.

We had been under the canopy for some days and had not seen the sun directly during that time; now we were up in the sky and had left the dim green world below us. Far to the south we could see the great barrier of mountains that forms the backbone of Sumatra, and all around us was a carpet of green, the tops of the trees that had until minutes before seemed so remote. We climbed all over "our" tree and made a few forays onto neighboring ones that could be reached along interlocked branches but toward sunset made our way back to our "elevator" and down to the ground for the night.

We later climbed other trees, always using the same method of getting up there, but truly saw little except the tree. It was years later that I managed finally to live in a tree as opposed to simply visiting one, so I cannot speak with authority about the life of or in the canopy in the jungles of the East. Nevertheless, I believe that the basic routine, if I may call it that, is probably the same in all jungles. I had supposed when I climbed up with Achi that there would be animals going in all directions, but this is apparently never the case—they follow definite routes aloft just as they do on the ground. Just how they choose these paths I don't know, though these do seem to include the major water holes between the main supporting branches. Some of these holes are relatively shallow basins, but others are veritable cisterns that go deep into the hollow trunks and contain pure water long after all other sources have dried up. Achi and I saw few animals of any size on our expeditions aloft, but it takes several days for them to get used to something as bizarre as pale-skinned bipeds that suddenly pop up in their territory. Once they do get used to you, they generally ignore you even when they are walking through "your" tree house; unless it's a band of monkeys, in which case they tend to help themselves to anything that looks edible or otherwise interesting. In South America, where I did live aloft for several weeks, they delighted in grabbing preserved specimens in bottles and hurling them to the ground some one hundred and twenty feet below!

Small animal life we did see in plenty, both in water holes and on batches of vegetation—snails, frogs, "bugs" by the millions, and one vermilion snake—but I had not attempted to carry collecting gear aloft and so did nothing but make a mental note that there is plenty of life in the trees and that a thorough collecting job should include an exhaustive search in the canopy. Many of the insects I had also seen on the ground, but some looked quite different from anything I remembered. I made no attempt to chase these, having no ambition to risk a hundred-foot fall onto the enormous flangelike buttress roots that surrounded the base of the tree.

I was not keen on staying up in a tree after sunset in the highlands of Sumatra. The days were generally warmer than down by the coast, but the nights were much cooler and a thunderstorm was always heard over the hills, the whole sky clouding over densely and bright blue lightning flickering all the time. (In one place we stayed, quite high up, I invariably expected to be struck by lightning, though I cannot say why. It had nothing to do with storms being closer and was apparently something about the general atmosphere of the place, which made even Achi nervous, though he was no more able to explain it than I.)

Our very primitive camp was comfortable enough, but I woke one morning convinced that something must be frightfully wrong. What I can only call an atrocious smell —something between rotten garlic and skunk cabbage after rain—pervaded the camp, and I yelled for Achi who arrived at the double. When I asked where the stench was coming from (I had a horrible feeling our meagre food supplies had somehow gone completely rotten overnight), he began to giggle rather nervously and led me a short distance from the camp to the spot where he had deposited his prize. It was a Gymnure (*Echinosoricinae*), an insectivore related to the Hedgehog, and just about as revolting a mammal as I know of. This was the larger species *(Gymnura)* found in Burma, Malaya, and Sumatra. All the Gymnures are rat-shaped, with long scaled and bristled tails and large heads with very long snouts bristling with whiskers and filled with very sharp teeth. The long-tailed species that Achi had found is black and white, though this specimen was so damaged that it was difficult to tell. Achi had noticed the care I lavished on the skulls of rats and thought I might be interested in the skull of this animal as well, for which I gave him proper commendation, but when we had dug out the skull it was badly splintered—apparently the animal had been killed by some type of deadfall trap—and I could not use it. The smell was awful and just about as lingering as skunk, but eventually wore off. Achi contended that it was not as bad as the Teledu *(Mydaus)*, a most evil-smelling badger (and thus related to the skunks, though not closely) found in the mountainous parts of Borneo, Sumatra, and Java. These are smallish animals, about fifteen inches long, with a tiny, fluffy bobble of a tail, dark brown except for a white stripe from the top of the head to the tail. The snout is piglike, and the muzzle can be twitched about. Like the skunk, it has glands by the anus and can project a really foul-smelling liquid for a considerable distance: it is apparently aware of its virtual invulnerability and trundles about quite fearlessly, resorting to extreme measures only when grossly provoked. But Achi lost the argument over which smelled worse when he admitted that the Teledu is readily tamed and sometimes kept as a pet. No one would keep a Gymnure around deliberately.

Our supplies truly having run out a few days later, we returned to civilization, and I was shortly invited to visit still another tobacco plantation. Here all the men and boys turned out to see me and soon became very interested. They wandered around looking for squirrels in the trees and called me when any were seen. At first my shooting was vile and I missed a lovely big black squirrel on a palm trunk, but it improved later and I returned with a pair of fine black and a pair of very fine brown and orange squirrels. After a siesta the natives brought me a fresh coconut to drink and a mat to sit on under a half-built house. They were much astonished to see me put iodine on my thumb, lacerated by a half-dead squirrel, but then just about everything I did seemed to astonish somebody.

Much of Sumatra is more or less straight up and down,

and this plantation was no exception. The best "hunting ground" was in a ravine at one edge of the planted area. Achi and I penetrated this by descending six hundred almost obliterated steps and caught some most marvelous bugs. At the bottom was a clear, rushing river and a tobacco shed in which we rested. The vegetation was secondary, dense and absolutely glorious. Huge palms, tall forest trees, exotic plants thirty feet tall, huge mosses, making cool shades and lighted holes like steaming ovens. We were crawling with huge chestnut-brown leeches, eaten alive by tiny mosquitoes and ants, and stung violently by huge-leafed, tall weeds. These stings remained for several days; they were not visible, but if touched, breathed on, put in water or the sun gave a burning, pricking, itching pain. We forced our way through *lallong** and then ascended the path, arriving after dark.

My host had one pet which, in a way, changed things considerably for me. This was Sambo, a Wow-Wow or Silvery Gibbon (*Hylobates moloch*), that I took for a walk each evening after tea. He had a long, light chain attached to a belt, and we visited the bushes and *lallong* at the bottom of the garden where he went twice a day to get food for himself. He ran along on his hind legs, holding the chain up and looking around every two seconds to see if I was following. He would immediately begin catching grasshoppers and beetles, which he ate sitting on my shoulder and holding onto my head. Gen-

---

*There is really no English translation for *lallong;* this is a very tall grass, higher than a man, generally wheatlike in appearance, but it has a flower on top that on going to seed looks like cotton and finally blows all over the place.

tle, entirely "human," and very quiet, he led me along, now climbing along posts, now sitting on my arm with his little arms softly around my neck, gazing into my face and uttering little whining "puffs" of noise. On our return to the house he sat in my chair while I read and smoked, licking his or my hand continuously for salt, parting my fingers or turning my hand over as required.

The Gibbon most commonly kept as a pet by the Malays is the so-called Agile Gibbon *(H. agilis)*, a redundant name if ever I heard one, for *all* gibbons are unbelievably agile [see Figure 13]. The Malays call them *Unka-putih* and treat them as members of the family, sometimes showing them more affection than they do their own children. The Wow-Wows are also quite common as pets, particularly a pale gray form from Java, and have been carried all over the islands for centuries, but still are represented by distinct subspecies despite all the possible mixing that could and probably has taken place. In captivity they are almost invariably docile and affectionate, though in the wild they are reported to be quite the reverse. I made no actual "studies" of any of the gibbons in the wilds, merely observing them as they swooped past or listening to their morning and evening chorales, but those who have studied them state that they are invariably nervous and excitable, and fight viciously with other groups of gibbons though they seem to be fairly peaceable within family groups. They can inflict really dreadful bites, their upper and lower canines being recurved and razor-sharp; and their attacks are lightning fast and usually premeditated. In fact, my host bore a scar on his hand, the result of a slashing bite inflicted by a previous pet gibbon he had offended in some way.

The gibbons are in many respects the most intelligent of the apes, enough so to carry grudges and wait for a suitable opportunity to take revenge, always when the victim is not expecting it. Sambo, though, was a prize example of these clean, gentle creatures, and I asked my host where I might be able to obtain one like him. He told me that I should try the nearby native market since they were occasionally available there, but that it was most unlikely that anyone would part with one already kept as a pet. Thereafter I haunted the market. I saw several but none seemed to match Sambo, who was then my standard of excellence among gibbons. Achi advised waiting until we went farther south and I reluctantly agreed.

I returned a number of times to the ravine, which was a truly lovely place—a clear stream flanked by vertical jade-green walls of short moss, with a similar gorge entering from the right, some six feet broad, partly choked by stones, and the whole merging upward with a canopy of dense, billowing vegetation from which rose one-hundred-foot smooth white shining trunks holding up a heaven of dark shimmering green, and entering this glade a glare of sunlight, dancing with golden butterflies. This river we crossed by a rough bridge and then ascended the opposite wall to another clearing. We rested on the way, observing monkeys out of range and squirrels disappearing before one could fire. From the top of this ledge we looked down over the ravine stretching to right and left for miles like a sea of billowing dark-green clouds from which issued every now and then the screaming laugh of hornbills, the croak of monkeys as they crashed through the trees, or the weird calls of various birds, echoing as if in a vast cave. We returned by the same path, shooting a squirrel and a fine tree shrew [see Figures 14 and 15] on the way.

The animals that most fascinated me in this ravine were a myriad of flying lizards *(Draco)*. I had seen these many times before, but here they seemed more common and somehow more colorful than elsewhere. The ravines and gorges were always filled with butterflies of brilliant hue, and I had been startled one day to see one arc across a clearing instead of lolloping about as butterflies do. Also, its wings fluttered in a most un-butterflylike manner, and I made my way as quickly as possible to the tree on which it had alighted, putting to flight dozens more of these beautiful creatures. As soon as they closed their wings they became virtually invisible, closely matching the color of the tree trunks on which they landed, but eventually I got close enough to take a really good look and discovered some interesting facts about them.

These flying lizards do not, of course, "fly" any more than the "flying" squirrels, snakes, frogs, and such do. All of these glide from one spot to another, and most have nothing more than a membrane stretched between the fore and hind legs. *Draco*, however, has "wings" that are not attached to the legs, and runs up tree trunks in normal lizard fashion rather than humping along like inchworms the way the Kaguan, for example, must do. Also, *Draco*'s front and hind legs are just about equal in length, unlike some other lizards (e.g., *Anolis*), which have very short front legs and long, much better muscled hind legs, looking like a miniature *Tyrannosaurus.*

These lovely little animals have three head appendages—a gular flap under the chin and a flap on each of the hind edges of the lower jaw. After they have reversed themselves on the tree trunk and are pointing downward, they constantly bob their heads about. If alarmed or if they spot food at a distance, they open their wings, extend the gular flap (which acts as a vane, like the upright fin on an airplane), and rush down the tree trunk, head up, and finally just let go of the trunk, though they continue "running" for a bit even after they are airborne.

There are about twenty species of *Draco,* of a variety of color combinations, often with a metallic sheen on the body at least. *D. volans* has wings of orange with black markings, while another species I saw was a vivid green with iridescent blue and black bands on its wings. They average about ten inches long, of which half is tail.

I was told of another "flying" lizard, though this apparently had only a kind of fringe or webbing round the body, legs, and tail,* and was not nearly as adept at sailing from tree to tree as little *Draco.* By some rather extraordinary acrobatics and collusion between Achi and me, we did manage finally to get one specimen which we carried back in triumph. Much later I acquired another species with no effort at all, but that was most unusual.

The other lizards that were common everywhere, and in fact are found over half the world, were various geckos. There are about 270 species in all, but I could not bring myself to pickle any of them. They are delightful little animals, and I spent many an hour watching one

---

*Presumably *Ptychozoon homalocephalum,* related to the Geckos. The fringe apparently acts both as camouflage and as a kind of parachute. [S. W. S.]

that lived somewhere in the wall of my room and came out to dash about the ceiling—upside down, of course—in search of insects in the evening. I had seen geckos in Mediterranean countries but still found it somewhat unnerving to see them walk up a perfectly vertical wall and then bend over and set out across the ceiling. They have very specialized feet, of course, but it was only very recently that the exact mechanism was figured out;* it is quite one thing for a fly weighing practically nothing to crawl about upside down, but some of the Eastern Geckos are up to fifteen inches long, and it seems unreasonable for an animal that size to defy gravity in this way.

The geckos are very regular in their habits, and those that take up residence in houses, which they often do, can be counted on to appear at the same time each evening. They become very tame, almost "domesticated," and there are many stories of geckos that have "turned up for dinner" when a family returns to a house vacated even for months. Some species are practically voiceless, though the Tokay Gecko *(Gekko gecko)* can produce a violent "startle reaction," as the doctors call it, with its stentorian bark *to kay,* particularly effective if one is nearly asleep or not quite awake. The Tokay Gecko is considered good luck by the Malays, though other species are thought by various native peoples to be deadly poisonous. In fact, none of the geckos is poisonous—their sole defense is to shed their tails, which are rather

---

*The undersides of the digits are equipped with pads that bear numerous microscopic hooks that catch on even the most minute irregularities in the surface; even glass is rough enough to afford a foothold. [S. W. S.]

brittle. So many that I saw were in the process of growing new ones that one must assume that they lead very adventurous lives.

My host had some interest in and knowledge of natural history, and he asked if I had visited the mangrove swamps along the coast. Of course I had seen these, but I admitted I had not actually been in one. He wrote down the name of a friend of his who lived in Medan and had a boat and would, he thought, be willing to take me down along the coast and then a bit inland along one of the great tidal rivers. I expressed myself as suitably grateful, and he proceeded to tell me something of these swamps which are found off sheltered bays and lagoons fed by rivers rich in silt and where there is tidal ebb and flow. These conditions favor trees rather than herbs [i.e., non-woody plants] but do require very special adaptations for root-breathing, and also result in a very specialized fauna. This last I was particularly keen to see.

On our return to Medan I called on my host's friend, presenting a letter of introduction he had given me, and explained who I was and what I was doing. He twinkled at me a bit and announced that he would be delighted to take me—not as a favor to his friend, but to my mother, whom he had met when she traveled in the East Indies! He would not hear of my staying at a hotel and promptly sent someone round to collect my bags and Achi and to pacify the hotel for my sudden departure, in the meantime showing me to my room and providing an elegant lunch impeccably served by several liveried "footmen."

During dinner he talked of just about everything under the sun except mangrove swamps, including in his discourse a lively account of his days at Cambridge that did nothing to prepare me for the fact that I might be expected to accomplish some work when I attended that august institution. After we had "repaired" to the verandah for coffee and excellent cigars, he made up for this lapse by giving me extremely precise instructions on what I should wear the next morning, i.e., my very oldest clothes, preferably some I wouldn't mind discarding afterward if necessary, with a long-sleeved shirt and a hat. I looked somewhat distressed at this last, since the hats I possessed would have been appropriate at Ascot or Lords [cricket grounds] but were hardly suitable for barging about in mangrove swamps. Even in the dim light he saw my consternation and promptly said he would lend me proper headgear and would also provide a hat for Achi. He declined, however, to let me take collecting gear with me, announcing with a cheerful grin that he wished to get back the same day. He also announced the hour at which he wished to start, and I bade him a rather hasty good-night.

Very early the next morning we set out in his small but comfortable boat, and after several hours he eased into a small cove and anchored. It seemed to me to be awfully far out, but he demurred at going further in and launched a tiny dinghy in which we rowed to the "shore." There really was no such thing, simply that the water became shallow enough so that we could step out onto, and into, the mud without drowning. This mud was like no other mud I have encountered, almost like liquid jelly and giving off a nearly visible stench, and the reason for the admonition that we should wear our oldest clothes became immediately apparent. We waded through this muck, continually slapping at mosquitoes, which showed marked ingenuity in finding any exposed portion of one's anatomy and seemed to me to be undeterred by the mosquito netting draped over my hat, until Achi noticed a gap in mine and tucked the netting further in under my collar. Mosquitoes here numbered in the millions; the sand flies came in billions and simply ignored the netting, sailing blithely through and grabbing a meal on the way. I wondered why I had wished to visit a mangrove swamp and gratefully accepted a cigar from my host. It was not like those he had offered me the night before, having been carefully selected for its ability to asphyxiate animal life in general. I shudder to think of its effect in a closed room; but nevertheless, its effect was only moderate here. We mushed on.

The first vegetation here consisted of groves of one genus of mangrove, *Rhizophora*, provided with extraordinary stilt roots that extend from the trunk. These interlacing supports form an almost impenetrable tangle and serve both to anchor the tree in the ever shifting mud and against the tides that wash it daily. The upper roots are exposed even at high tide and are provided with special pores called lenticels that enable the tree to breathe.

These outer mangrove swamps are truly neither land nor water, and the trees bear seeds that germinate while still attached to the parent plant, sending out a large primary root. The seeds float when they do drop and may be carried away by the tide, but if they drop directly onto the mud, they land in such a position that the root becomes buried in the mud and, within hours apparently, sends out secondary rootlets that anchor the seedling. Further in, another genus of mangroves takes over, sending out long snakelike roots across the mud, but still in a tangle, and finally a nearly "dry land" genus that mingles with palms and other plants in areas where the tide has little effect.

There was mud everywhere. Things scuttled and scratched and made little plopping noises all around—crabs hurrying out of our path and darting into water-filled holes, tiny crustaceans, and a curious fish that behaved rather like a frog. This last was *Periophthalmus* ["eyes outside"], known locally as the mud-skipper. Its eyes are close together on top of the head, can be moved quite readily, and protrude like those of a frog. Its pectoral fins and tail are especially strong, and it hops about on the surface in search of the tiny crustaceans it eats. In fact, it cannot stay long under water. Its breathing apparatus is very specialized. It collects water in cavities on each side of the head, and these keep the gills moist, more or less the equivalent of using an aqualung on land. I was told that one could drown them by holding them under water for a time, but, apart from not wishing to experiment in this fashion, I would have had difficulty in acquiring a specimen with my bare hands. When alarmed they leaped for considerable distances and had far less trouble getting about on the mud than we did. I wanted to try to measure one of these leaps—leaping fishes being something beyond my previous experience—but the mud was so liquid that they left no measurable impress and we could only estimate. One particularly acrobatic individual, dislodged by a root hurled at him by Achi, made a jump we judged to be over two feet. Inasmuch as these are very small fish, about the size of a govie, this is no mean feat, but I was even more astonished to see

one suddenly stand up on its tail! I was sorely tempted
to take my glasses off to clean them, but I had by now
nothing on me that was not soaked and mud-spattered
or worse. The mud-skipper had almost immediately subsided into its normal position, and I was not certain I had
other witnesses to this extraordinary event and so looked
cautiously round. My host was more or less doubled up
with silent laughter, but recovered himself sufficiently to
tell me that this is quite ordinary behavior for these fish.
He added that he had not told me ahead of time, since,
of course, I would not have believed him. He was right;
I wouldn't have. Why they do it has apparently never
been satisfactorily determined. In its way this fish takes
the place of the amphibians that would ordinarily inhabit
such swamps but cannot exist here because of the salt
water.

The little crabs that darted about were Fiddler Crabs
(*Uca*) and were hilarious to watch. We lay down on the
most solid bit of mud we could find, one dotted with
clumps of coarse grass, but fairly liquid all around, so
that we were more or less on a level with the animal life
around us, and then concentrated on one of the tiny
"burrows." After we had been quiet a while, an eye appeared, perched on top of its stalk and waving a bit as it
looked for danger in its vicinity. When the eye was assured that all was serene, the crab, about the size of an
English penny [old style, presumably, roughly the size of
a silver dollar], sidled carefully out, still waving its eyes
and now beckoning to us with its large white claw. At eye
level this produced the giggles in all of us, but we were
roused by a sudden splashing somewhere off to our left.
We got up rather quickly, for my host had warned me of

various horrors to be encountered in the mangrove swamps, not the least of which is the very dangerous saltwater crocodile *(Crocodylus porosus)* that haunts the swamps and is more feared by the natives than any shark. Fortunately, I never saw one, and we did not see the animal that had done the splashing. It could have been an otter, though these seem to be nocturnal. Of course, it could have been old *Crocodylus,* too; we did not investigate. Wild pigs also visit the swamps to root for crabs and mollusks, but either we were there at the wrong time of day, or we were too far out for these since we saw no sign of them. Of crows, squabbling over bits of carrion, we saw plenty, and a lone Fish Eagle *(Haliaetus leucogaster?)* soared overhead. There were many other birds, glittering in their brilliant plumage against the green of the mangroves and the lucent blue of the sky, and we heard macaques somewhere behind us, yelling at each other over choice morsels. I saw these Crab-eating Macaques in Bali and elsewhere, but on this day they eluded us.

We puttered about for some time but finally made our way back to the dinghy, which was now lying on the mud, and by pushing and hauling, got it back into navigable water. A much shorter trip got us back to the boat, my host making the unnecessary observation, "Tide going out, y'know."

I had visions of making the boat permanently uninhabitable, since all three of us were sodden and covered with stinking mud, but my host soon made it clear that he had no intention of allowing his spotlessly clean little launch to be contaminated in this fashion. Securing the line from the dinghy to a convenient stanchion, he proceeded to peer at the sea all around with intense concen-

tration—looking for *C. porosus*, no doubt—and finally
announced that Achi and I should jump in and flail about
until we had divested ourselves of every vestige of mud
from the swamp. This we did more than willingly, and
when we had completed our ablutions, he did the same
while we sat in the dinghy. Back on board, he had us strip
and wring out our clothes, hanging them over the taffrail
to dry. We all donned wonderfully comfortable and colorful batik native cloths and retired to the cabin, where
he produced lunch in short order, including some lemonade of a really startling hue!

That evening, once more impeccably dressed (for a
European at least), I borrowed a bicycle from my host
and for the sheer fun of it toured around the colorful
native quarters of Medan, watching these cheerful, un-
hurried, handsome people as they bartered in the markets, played their games in open areas, and generally
milled about the streets. I had turned into a fairly narrow
street well off the main thoroughfare when I skidded to
a halt. There, looking incredibly forlorn and mangy and
tied with a pittance of rope, was a Wow-Wow. She, for
it proved to be a female, looked at me and I at her, and
I roared for the owner. This individual, a scruffy and
wizened man of indeterminate age and ancestry, shuffled
out of his shop which, from what I could see, was also a
disgrace. There followed a somewhat complicated
palaver, further confused by the almost immediate as-
semblage of a very watchful crowd that gathered round.

When I demanded to know if the Wow-Wow belonged
to him, he bowed obsequiously and whined that it was his
"friend and companion." I proceeded to berate him in
no uncertain terms and in several languages, for the

poor creature was really in terrible condition and I was frankly shocked by the contrast between this and the other pet gibbons I had seen. I asked him what he wanted for her, and he pretended to look appalled by the suggestion that he should sell her, but I noticed a rather crafty look in his eyes and pressed my suit. "Nona," for so I had already named her—the Malay name for a pretty girl— was going to be mine if love or money could manage it. When neither seemed to be producing any results, I changed my tactics and threatened to call "the authorities," hinting that I knew all sorts of dreadful things about him and would certainly see to it that he would be severely punished if he did not immediately hand over the obviously mistreated animal, in which case I would magnanimously ignore his other misdeeds.

He was a bit taken aback by this—presumably because I was, quite by chance, on the right track, as evidenced by murmurings from the previously quiet but definitely expectant crowd, which I now sensed was on my side. Thus fortified, I continued my onslaught, and informed him that in fact I would not pay him anything and would take the gibbon whether he liked it or not. By now he was looking distinctly nervous, though he maintained his generally calm outward appearance, and continued to whine and mutter. Finally, addressing him with some of my best Anglo-Saxon monosyllables, I grabbed the rope, which broke, and "Nona" leaped to my shoulder. I re-mounted my bike and, after glowering once more at the shopkeeper, set off as elegantly as I could toward home. The crowd cheered and laughed and then simply evaporated, leaving me a deserted street and the fading and less than assured ravings of that "gentleman." Nona gave him one last look and a peculiar hoot that I never heard from her again. It was in some subtle way the most menacing sound I had ever heard.

Once out into the central part of Medan my anger, which had simmered while I pedaled along, subsided, and Nona and I began to get acquainted, much to the amusement and delight of the natives we passed. We must have made an interesting spectacle, me in my London-tailored suit and hat—I lacked only a furled umbrella to complete the picture—with a gibbon entwined around my neck. I began to be somewhat unsure of the reception I would get from my host, but he was apparently proof against any kind of alarum or excursion. When I entered the drawing room with Nona, he looked up and said, more or less, "I say, scruffy-looking beast. Where did you get it?"

I stammered out the whole story of my search for a gibbon and started to apologize for inflicting Nona on him, but he stopped me with a wave of his hand. "Think I know the creature. Wretched man. Ought to be shot, keeping a gibbon like that. Better take her to Achi. Those chaps know what to do for them. Got mange or something. Make splendid pets."

So take her to Achi I did. Achi was a perfect light golden-brown, but when he had taken a good look at Nona, who sat quietly while he examined her, he looked not only grim but a curious almost greenish color, and I thought of the stories of *Orang Blundas* who had not returned from Achin, and was more grateful than ever to his father for his extraordinary hospitality. But he soon calmed down and informed Nona directly that she need not fear, he would take care of her.

We sat down and had a palaver, since I wanted to go on to Java, if only for a brief rest (!), but was not sure I could cart both Achi and a frankly ill gibbon around with me. Achi settled this by stating that he would go home for a short time, taking Nona with him, and that he could get to Java easily—he didn't say how, but the way he said it brooked no argument—and would meet me there.

Cure her Achi did, and the three of us became the closest of friends. Nona wore a belt to which we attached a long, very light chain. This she gathered up and held in one hand as she wobbled along on her hind legs when we went walking. She collected insects for me—and incidentally the British Museum—and was much more efficient than I was. She would move systematically along a fallen tree trunk, loosening the bark and probing beneath it, finding all manner of splendid specimens which she handed to me or Achi. She would continue to collect a particular species until we closed the lid on the collecting bottle, and then she ate any others *of that species* which she found! If she found another species, we went through the same routine. It was utterly uncanny, and I cannot explain it. She did other things that defy normal explanation, and which puzzled even Achi who looked on her as nearly a person.

Thus ended my first visit to Sumatra.

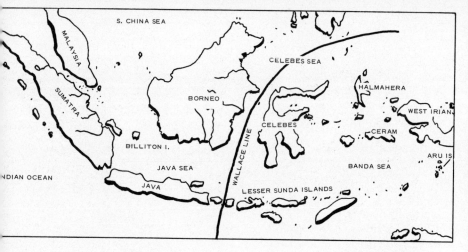

Figure 1. Indonesia, showing Wallace's Line. This latter has been amended in recent years because of more detailed studies of the distribution of animals in the islands.

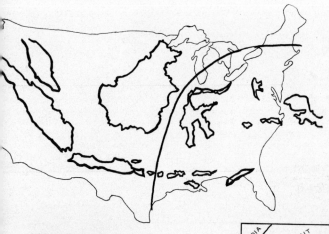

Figure 2. Indonesia, superimposed on the United States to show the really vast extent and size of the islands.

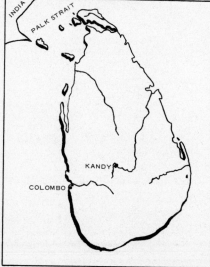

Figure 3. Ceylon.

Figures 4 & 5. Slender Loris, awake and asleep.
Pencil drawings.

Figure 6. Malaya.

Figure 7. Petros leaps over the log. Redrawn from an illustration in Mystery Schooner (published under the nom-de-plume Terence A. Roberts, but with "Illustrations by Ivan T. Sanderson"!).

Figure 10. Sumatra and the Mentawi Islands,
with inset showing the general topography.

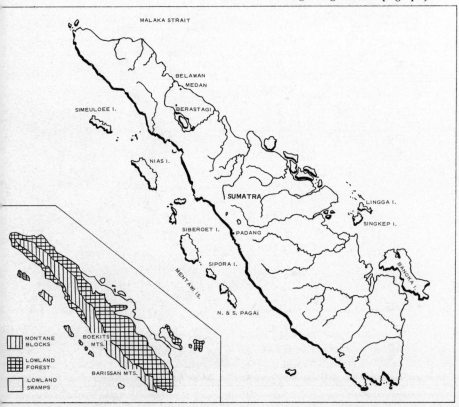

MALAKA STRAIT

BELAWAN
MEDAN
BERASTAGI

SIMEULOEE I.

NIAS I.

SUMATRA

LINGGA I.

SINGKEP I.

SIBEROET I. PADANG

SIPORA I.

BANGKA I.

MENTAWI IS.

N. & S. PAGAI

MONTANE
BLOCKS

LOWLAND
FOREST

LOWLAND
SWAMPS

BOEKITS
MTS.

BARISSAN MTS.

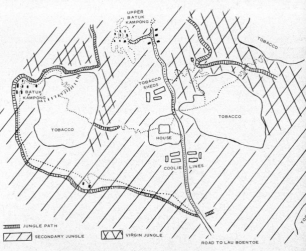

Figure 11. Map of the Lau Boentoe Estate, traced from the original in Ivan Sanderson's diary. The dotted line shows his various routes round the estate.

UPPER BATUK KAMPONG

TOBACCO

BATUK KAMPONG

TOBACCO SHEDS

TOBACCO

TOBACCO

HOUSE

COOLIE LINES

IIIIIII JUNGLE PATH

//// SECONDARY JUNGLE

\/\/\/ VIRGIN JUNGLE

ROAD TO LAU BOENTOE

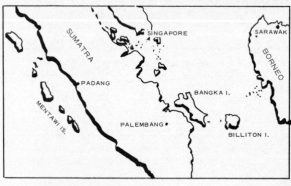

SUMATRA

SINGAPORE

SARAWAK

BORNEO

PADANG

BANGKA I.

MENTAWI IS.

PALEMBANG

BILLITON I.

Figure 12. Southern Sumatra and Billiton Island.

Figure 13. The Hoolock (Hylobates hoolock), one of the typical Gibbons. Pen and ink and brush. Ivan seems never to have drawn a Siamang or a Wow-Wow.

Figures 14 & 15. Feather-tailed
(previously, Pen-tailed) Tree Shrew
(Ptilocercus lowi). Pencil drawing
compared with pen and ink and
brush, the former done about 1940,
the latter about 1956.

There are two basic "kinds" of
tree shrews, the Feather-tails, and the
Tupaias, which constitute a separate
sub-family. The "tree shrew"
mentioned in the text could have
been any one of a large number of
species of Tupaias found in this
area. They represent our earliest
"ancestors." For more on this, the
reader is referred to The Monkey
Kingdom, which, incidentally, Ivan
considered his best book.

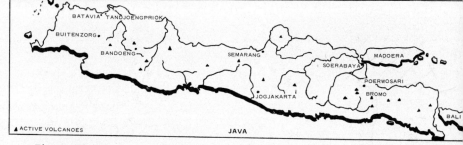

Figure 16. Java.

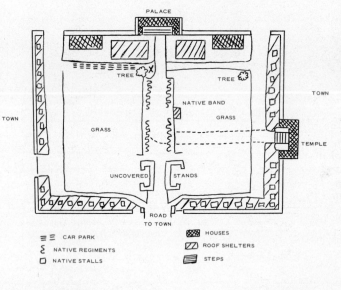

Figure 17. Plan of the Sultan's Palace grounds at Djokja (now Jogjakarta), traced from the original sketch in the diary.

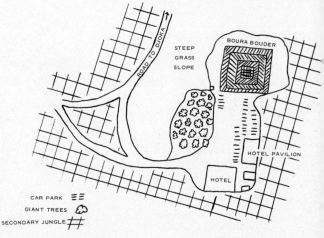

Figure 18. Boura Bouder and its environs, traced from the original in the diary.

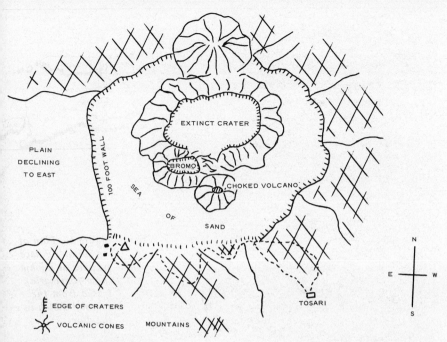

PLAIN
DECLINING
TO EAST

100 FOOT WALL

EXTINCT CRATER

BROMO

CHOKED VOLCANO

SEA

OF

SAND

TOSARI

N

E — W

S

⊨ EDGE OF CRATERS

✳ VOLCANIC CONES

MOUNTAINS ✕✕✕

*Figure 19. The Bromo and
its environs. The broken
line indicates the path
followed by Ivan. Again,
traced from the original in
his diary.*

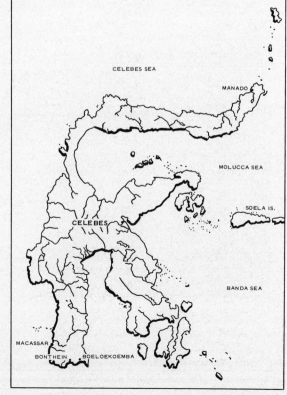

CELEBES SEA

MANADO

MOLUCCA SEA

SOELA IS.

CELEBES

BANDA SEA

MACASSAR

BONTHEIN   BOELOEKOEMBA

Figure 20. Celebes.

Figure 21. The Babirusa. Pencil drawing.

Figure 22. Pencil drawing of an unidentified young man. Although his "people" tend to be somewhat stylized, portraits are meticulously detailed.

Figure 23. Ivan's "universal cat"; from the text of the notebook in which this appeared, it was apparently intended to be a puma! One must be grateful to Achi.

*Figures 24 & 25. These are apparently the original drawings of the
Cutty Sark and the stag's head mentioned in the text; the racing
tout seems not to have survived, or it may have been given away.
Both are in pencil.*

Figure 26. *Ternate and Halmahera, with neighboring islands; inset shows Bali and its eastern neighbors.*

Figure 27.
The Aru Islands.

Figure 28. *A Cuscus (Phalanger), but not necessarily the "model" that invaded Ivan's bed. Pencil drawing.*

Figures 29 & 30. Tube-nosed
Fruit Bat in flight, and
detailed drawing of the head.
Both in pencil.

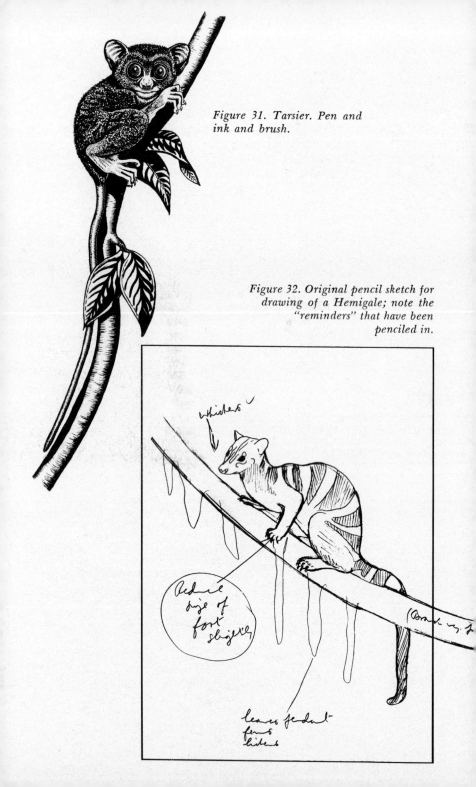

Figure 31. Tarsier. Pen and ink and brush.

Figure 32. Original pencil sketch for drawing of a Hemigale; note the "reminders" that have been penciled in.

8

Singapore and Java; Palaces and Volcanic Craters

DESPITE THE ACTUALLY very short distance separating Sumatra from Java, I had to go to Singapore to get a boat for Java. Thus I rushed to Belawan just in time to catch the boat for Singapore, which we reached the next morning. The approach is very interesting, through a sea of low, long, rugged islands. We took on a pilot several miles out and entered the vast harbor through an amazingly narrow gully, flanked by red cliffs and covered with vegetation more to be expected in southern England. The sky also looked English, being heavy with rain and the air cool, with every now and then drizzling rain. There are miles of docks and hundreds of huge boats of all nations, while in the next bay at the other end of the town are thousands of native sampans and praus. We tied up after

much maneuvering behind a Bibi Liner alongside the
wharf. There was a huge crowd of Malays and Tamils
aboard and a corresponding crowd to meet them. I
handed my luggage over to the Europe Hotel's man and
dashed off by taxi to this hotel to book a room.

Much of my time during the few days I spent in Singapore had to be devoted to "courtesy visits," which
varied from charming to ghastly, but were sometimes
useful. On one occasion I was wearing my O.E. [Old
Etonian] tie and suddenly saw another one approaching
me. We immediately asked each other to lunch and had
a great talk. He advised me to go to see Boden Kloss, the
director of the Raffles Museum. This I did, taking my
[British] Museum letter with me. Luckily, I ran into this
gentleman in the galleries, and he told me to wait in his
room. He was very helpful and interesting, and when I
had explained myself and my needs, he asked for my
letter and some hours of time with which to collect me
some letters of introduction for Java. He introduced me
to the curator and assistant curator, and together we
discussed mammals (their chief study) for some time.
They said they would order some traps for me and gave
me many very useful tips on trapping, etc. I returned to
the hotel well satisfied.

The next morning I dressed hurriedly and finished my
packing. After an early breakfast in my room I dashed off
to the Museum, where I was met by the curator, Boden
Kloss having gone to Kuala Lumpur unexpectedly. He
had left a whole wad of letters and scientific papers on
Javanese mammals for me, besides three dozen very efficient traps. There are heaven knows how many kinds of
traps but, for the serious collector, either a good, solid,

light, and simple breakback or cage trap, or both, are most serviceable. Among breakbacks all that should be required is something to hold the bait and something else to hit the quarry squarely, neatly, and suddenly. Among the best of these is one trap that almost every collector must know. It is called a Scheiler or Schyler or whatever is best suited to the language of the country in which it is sold. I don't know where they are manufactured; mine were bought from a Chinese in Singapore and were second-hand. All Schylers seem to be second-hand; they never break and they hit so hard and so suddenly that they seldom get carried away even by the largest animals. As you will see, I had trouble with mine initially, but they may have been misused by their previous owner. Considering the price I paid for them, I can't complain much.

Having sent all my luggage on by the hotel man, I made my good-byes and arrived in pouring rain in plenty of time to catch the tender. This was a very rowdy motor pinnace which stopped on the way at a tiny cargo boat for no apparent reason before taking us on to the steamer, which was a medium-sized boat of superb comfort, altogether more like a yacht, spotlessly clean as are all Dutch boats, and with excellent service and cuisine.

The trip took several days, and we stopped briefly at Billiton, a small island off the southeast extremity of Sumatra, beyond Bangka. There are extensive tin mines on both islands. Billiton is mostly flat and covered with dense palm jungle; there are, however, four or five extinct volcanic peaks just visible in the distance. The bay is very large, the anchorage being well over a mile out. Several large praus, three steam tugs, and a lot of motor boats came out to the boat, and a tremendous amount of cargo was discharged and stowed in an amazingly short time. A tender crowded with native passengers came out also. Shortly after anchoring, the dense squall that had been lurking on the horizon descended on us; it began to blow quite hard and rain slightly; and so, after waving good-bye to my erstwhile cabin mate in a wildly tossing steam pinnace, I retired to bed feeling very bad—probably due to the violent smell of bad fish that permeated the place as soon as the holds were opened.

The next morning found us entering the harbor at Tandjoengpriok, the port for Batavia. I stayed in Batavia for nearly a week, accomplishing "nothing," not because of sloth but because of the hospitality of everyone I met. I was wined and dined and taken on numerous local sight-seeing trips, to bird markets, and the like, and frankly gave up any idea of trying to do any collecting here.

In any case, the truly wild areas in Java are rather few, this island having been thickly populated and highly civilized for millennia. The British Museum was not interested in rats and mice caught in houses, and I was not after large mammals—one of the interesting "relics" in Java is the so-called Javan Rhinoceros (*Rhinocerus sondaicus*), but they were rare even when I was in Java, and I had little hope of seeing one. Insects, of course, are found everywhere, but Java has been extensively "collected"; thus I chose to take a holiday from this also.

One side trip to Bandoeng for a weekend was not without incident, though this was not zoological in nature. We flew in one of the large three-engined monoplanes that run both ways to Bandoeng and Semarang twice a day and are always full. They seat eight comfortably, ten at a pinch. The luggage was stowed in a compartment beneath the cockpit and behind the passengers' accommodation, which was airy, spacious, and provided with windows and cane armchairs. The takeoff was graceful and the whole run very smooth, except for a bit on each side of the mountain ranges when a little movement was felt. The view was gorgeous—first, over the plains, an alternation of tiny *kampongs* and paddy fields in every shade of green strongly contrasted with the red of the houses, clearings, and roads, and the yellow of the rivers; and later the hills and mountains covered with soft-looking trees and very plainly showing the system of denudation by stream, brook, rivulet, and river; next a plain of larger paddy fields; and then suddenly we descended and flew for some miles below the clouds and then landed easily at the Bandoeng airfield.

My host here was a Scot, popularly called "Wee," and we spent the weekend at fancy-dress balls and general carousing. The morning of my departure I was aroused at about five thirty and immediately got up, dressed, and packed my bag. "Wee" provided vast cups of coffee, and at six o'clock we set out by taxi for the flying field, killing a large hen very neatly on the way. The usual efficiency at the station got me into the plane quickly, and sharp at six thirty we left. We flew over the plateau at fairly low altitude, but just near the mountains we entered a dense cloud bank for some ten minutes, after which the pilot seemed to lose his way, and we circled around for about an hour between the hills. I then fell asleep and on waking found him following a railway line that seemed to go the wrong way, so he branched off and maneuvered endlessly, at last making a forced landing on an emergency field some forty miles to the west of our track and halfway to Batavia. He had run out of fuel. So we all got out and sat or strolled about for an hour while the pilot went some ten miles to a town to get more fuel, there being no telephone at the field. A huge crowd of natives gathered to "look," like all other human beings. Finally a taxi appeared with eight tins of fuel, which were put into the plane through an inlet pipe on the top of the single thick wing. Just before this was finished, another plane appeared and landed, taxiing along to us. A very efficient Javanese pilot and a mass of mechanics appeared who thoroughly slated our man and bundled us into the new plane. We took off straightaway, flew quickly between the mountains, over Buitenzorg, and landed at Batavia without any circling around, just in time for lunch. Thereafter I stuck to land transport!

I traveled by train to Djokja [Jogjakarta], sending my heavy luggage on to Soerabaya to await my arrival there. On the train a very pleasant Japanese gentleman took me under his wing and got me quickly away in the hotel bus when we reached Djokja. I was much amused at his way of dealing with the "boys" who demanded more money: he gave them each one cent more, without so much as the movement of one muscle of his face. He also got me a good room at the hotel, which was almost fully booked.

Later he introduced me to a friend of his, also Japanese, who told us that he had received an invitation from the Sultan of all the Javanese to attend an official court with the Dutch Resident and other notables, as head of the Japanese community and an important person, and very kindly asked us to join him. He picked us up the next morning in a kind of rudimentary brougham drawn by two little native ponies, and we rode along the main street toward the palace which forms one end behind an enormous grass-covered square. Literally thousands of Javanese were flocking along the street, dressed in sombre dark blues, blacks, and browns, but with the most wonderful jewelry—vast diamond and silver earrings, gold necklaces, buttons, and large pieces of precious metals studded with jewels in exotic patterns in their beautiful glossy black, neatly made-up hair. As a whole, they are far darker-skinned than the Sundanese and on the average of shorter stature.

We got out of the vehicle at the gates of the square and began walking around to the right where there were innumerable "merry-go-rounds" and stalls selling sarongs and jewels, but mostly foodstuffs and every conceivable kind of toy painted in the brightest colors possible. Hundreds of children were about, spending their money on violently colored drinks called by their itinerant vendors *bir* and *susu,** or trumpets, whistles, rattles, moving wooden figures, little birds you wind up, flags and other emblematic toys. Hundreds of beautiful little women weighed down with native jewelry strutted gracefully about, while the men, laughing and talking, crowded into the "opera" given in well-guarded tents. With all of this there was, astonishingly enough, no "crowd smell" at all among these lovely people.

We found seats ["X" on the plan, Figure 17] near the

---

*Beer and milk, respectively. Possibly the milk was artificially colored—the Malays seem to prefer "violently colored" drinks; or Ivan got the vendors mixed. [S. W. S.]

"reviewing stand" when the procession began. The minor princes came first, attended by the chief men of their families and a varying number of retainers carrying their possessions which signify superiority—silver urns and boxes, gold crowns, and trays of fruits and such—and all beautifully dressed. Then came the absolutely superlative rajah-prince, at least six foot seven in height and proportionately heavy, with a gold headdress, gold-braided trousers, sumptuous black and gold and silver sarong, diamond and emerald rings that could be seen even at one hundred yards, and an enormous sword literally covered with cut and uncut jewels. He walked beneath a vast gold sunshade carried by two boys, with a gorgeously arrayed relative on each side. He alone wore shoes, all the rest of his vast retinue, all dressed alike, going barefoot. Every kind of treasure followed him. Once he was ensconced in his pavilion before the palace, the Dutch Resident appeared followed by about a hundred cars carrying various dignitaries, all in full dress, the civilians wearing black tailcoats of evening design with white gloves and top hats, the women dressed as for a formal garden party. Finally, from the palace came a native marching band and four native regiments, which marched slowly to their places along the avenue. After various ceremonies, all the dignitaries repaired to the temple, and the crowd dispersed.

After lunch I drove off in a car provided by my friend's friend, all taxis having a holiday, to see the Boura Bouder [see Figure 18]. Going toward the mountains, we left the main road and entered more wooded and typically tropical country. Our first stop was at a small rectangular-based pyramid with two large and beautifully carved

Buddhas facing each other. The next was at the top of
the lawn-covered hill on which stands the marvelous
stepped pyramid hidden beneath a mass of carving. It
was a fete day here also, and a hurdy-gurdy and a lot of
native stalls had been placed under some truly giant
trees. The base of this wonderful monument is a broad,
flat platform, on which rise three vast "steps," each with
a high wall on its outside edge. The whole is covered
with carvings of gods, etc. It was first discovered by an
Englishman and in 1902 was entirely pulled down and
was rebuilt by 1914. I got a guide, a very pleasant Dutchman, who took me around the first step and showed me
the carved life history of Buddha running right around,
which he rattled off in very bad English. We then ascended to the top and sat down for a time. The guide was
also a sort of local policeman and told me he had constantly to move the Malays off the place. We came upon
a lot of natives sitting exchanging money there, which
they consider lucky. On descending to the hotel, another
police officer came over and shook hands with us and
said in Dutch that seventeen people had been arrested
there for letting off fireworks. I was then consulted as to
the proper English for a notice "THE LETTING OFF OF
FIREWORKS IS STRICTLY PROHIBITED."

It rained like billy-ho on the way back to Djokja, but
it stopped after dinner, and I went out for a short stroll
before going to bed, with the awful prospect of getting
up at five o'clock the next morning. I didn't quite manage this, but I did catch the train for Soerabaya. We
arrived there at about one thirty, and getting my few
bags out onto the platform, I began looking about for the
great Pat Lawrence with whom I was to stay. I soon easily

spotted him pushing through the crowd, a very tall, good-looking Englishman with a charming smile, dressed in a very smart gray-flannel suit. He had with him an equally tall and efficient boy who dealt with all my luggage, while we drove off to his palatial house in a car worthy of Croesus. Lunch was a perfectly cooked and served repast worthy of the Ritz, eaten from a circular polished table about ten feet in diameter and made of one solid piece of teakwood. The silver and flowers and army of boys in a smart navy-blue-and-white livery gave me the sense of great luxury. Mindful of things to come, I soaked it up as best I could.

After a couple of days of luxury I decided suddenly one morning to go to the Bromo that day. We looked up the trains, and I found that one left for Poerwosari at 12:15 P.M. Accordingly I rushed off and packed some things, and Lawrence's efficient boy got me settled in a first-class carriage. The journey was short and through paddy fields all the way. At Poerwosari I easily procured a good taxi but was unable to direct him, as I had a vague idea that there were two hotels for the Bromo. When we stopped at the other end of the town to fill up with petrol, I got hold of a Chinese (they all speak English), from whom I learned that the Bromo hotel was beyond Tosari, whereas I had told the driver to go to the hotel for the Bromo *in* Tosari. Then off we went along a creditable road. However, we had to take a succession of narrow byways at one point because the recent heavy rains had caused a part of the banking of Java loam to fall away. We made for a huge, gently sloping mountain that disappeared up into the clouds. The road was most interesting; I noticed that all the natives live in large communities surrounded by a stout bamboo fence and internally divided by a maze of the same. The natives here were Madarese, and for the most part still Hindu. They are very beautiful, dark skinned and bluish round the eyes like Hindus. Their likeness to the latter is accentuated in the women by the way they do their hair, quite different from the other Malay races.

After ascending some three hundred feet the road began to twist and turn and the air became chillier. Houses stopped and the road became a succession of hairpin bends. The driver was excellent and we ascended at a good pace; he took the bends without slackening speed, with a few inches to spare on the inside. All the way up the road is bordered by a row of stout trees at six-foot intervals on the outside, but nowhere are there alarming precipices. Once we stopped at a village to get more water, and I noticed with interest that the fenced kampong, being an impossibility, was abandoned, and that the bright silks had given way to stout warm batiks. The vegetation now changed to alpine, with queer five-needled pines and heavy-leafed bushes covered with gigantic trumpetlike white flowers. We now entered the clouds, like a very damp mist, and constantly came upon places where the inner bank of the road had fallen down and was either being dug off by natives or leveled if a large fall. Once the car had to pass through a mud slush up to the axles. The men working had only scanty clothes, although I was feeling the cold intensely. Tosari is one long street entered by such a sharp turning that the car had to back up twice, and it runs along the ridge of one mountain and around behind another. It is bordered by a lot of wooden shops and houses with tin roofs. We ascended another steep bit of road to the Bromo hotel, where I was cordially welcomed by the proprietor. After dinner I strolled around the place and looked down on the lights of Tosari. It was very cold and absolutely silent up there, with vast valleys all around banded by mist.

As arranged, I was awakened at 3:15 A.M. and managed in some extraordinary way to get up immediately. I was in a vile temper, as it was very cold, and the boy had only tapped on the door and then had gone off without giving me any light or food. Consequently, I had to start dressing by the light from the passage shining through my open door. The manager soon turned up fully dressed and I almost bit him in the neck, whereupon he rushed off to return shortly with a boy and a light and some indifferent coffee. I complained again and got some milk and a banana. Having dressed and donned my burberry, I started off for a long ride on a little mountain pony, with an old Malay guide bearing a torch and a tin of breakfast leading me.

We ascended a steep path through a little village where even at this hour the people were going out to work. They asked us if we were going to the Bromo and walked beside us for some way. The path twisted and turned, following the edges of ravines, ascending by the sides of the arms of the hills crossing from mountain to mountain along the top of colossal dykes, but always ascending. The vegetation became scrubby and grassy, the only tall trees being a kind of black-barked, long-thin-needle pine. The path soon narrowed down to a "one-man" track. There were no signs of habitation or cultivation up there, but up every main hill and down every main gorge wound a well-built path. We were always on the brink of one or two almost perpendicular declivities filled with these pines. The geological formation of these mountains seemed to be lava resting on volcanically raised metamorphic schists and overlaid with a very thick covering of every variety of volcanic ash, breccias, and earth. Landslides seemed to be constant.

After about two hours riding we arrived at a spot where two seats had been placed, just as dawn was breaking. This spot is on the edge of a vast extinct crater some twelve miles broad [see Figure 19], which now has a level surface of fine sand within. In the midst of this plain stand several volcanic cones of which one is active (the Bromo) and one is dormant. All around, the lip of the original crater is obvious, and the radiating valleys like that which we ascended are just like those seen in miniature on the Bromo itself. On the left-hand side a flat plain slopes gently away to the east as far as the eye can see, between the mountains. This does not merge with the sand sea but is separated by a drop (down to the latter) of about one hundred feet and almost perpendicular. As the sun rose with pale, yellowish, cold, misty light over the farther mountains, the pall of white mist lying on the sand sea glowed white, while out of it rose the regular volcanic peaks and from the Bromo a slowly billowing pillar of white steam, forever changing shape, but oh how slowly. The hills beyond lay quiet and gray-blue with drifting wraiths of cloud, and beyond these, again to the east, above a cloud bank appeared peaks, some crowned with tufts of volcanic smoke. Close at hand the deathly stillness was accentuated by the silent fringes of cloud that crept up the Tosari side of the mountains and down into the craters, clinging to the earth like ghostly paws.

I rode on almost immediately for another hour along the outside edge of the crater curving in and out along the sides of the lava flow gorges and eventually arrived at the highest point. We left the horses tethered by "Welkom," a small wooden shack, and did the last fifty feet on foot and had breakfast, shivering the whole time. In the dark, the lights of Poerwosari and Soerabaya had been visible while ascending, but now the whole plain was obscured by a cloud bank which we were far above. All the trees were stunted here, and the grass was like that of the Scottish Highlands. I noticed two little native houses below the path at the top of the hill, which has a rectangular altar-shaped stone on its summit. We then descended to the first stopping place and then took a lower road that followed the Tosari gorge all the way down. This is a very well constructed small road having an easy gradient throughout. We left this at the bottom of the ridge we were following and, striking across it by a tiny narrow path, mostly steps, we arrived at the hotel down the upper village path.

From there I returned to Soerabaya where I collected Achi, rounded up all my possessions, and took ship for Bali.

9

Bali: A Princess; Monkeys; Bats; and an Odd Crater

L UCKILY I AWOKE AT SIX
thirty, as I was not called, and managed to get packed
and ready by the time we dropped anchor off the almost
obscured town of Boeleleng. The steward helped me to
get my baggage into a huge gig rowed by three men with
another fellow sculling in the stem, and Achi followed,
somewhat impeded by his own bags and by Nona, who
was clinging to his neck. She did not take to sea travel at
all; but apparently, like humans, gibbons do not die of
mal de mer, they just wish they could.

Once ashore I met Phatima, the royal princess of Bali,
a large, very cheery woman, completely unshy, very polite and cultured, dressed in a sarong and a jade-green
imitation silk tunic with vast gold buttons. She was the
only remaining wife of the rajah conquered by the Dutch

in 1912 and had returned to the island after the war
[World War I]. At the time I met her, she owned all the
silver trade, a lot of land, a fleet of cars for hire, most of
the brasswork, etc. Since it was not my intention to do
any serious collecting here, I suggested that Achi take a
few days off while I tour the island in one of Phatima's
cars. He agreed with somewhat suspicious alacrity, and
an hour or so later I began the 114-kilometer drive
[roughly 75 miles] across the island to Denpasar. The
perfect day made the island look ideal. All the way along
every road streams of bronze-colored natives walked carrying vast loads on their heads (one woman as many as
thirty earthenware pots of considerable size). The country is very thickly populated, and nearly the whole of it
is beautifully constructed paddy fields, in which crowds
of people are working, ploughing with buffalo or the
beautiful ochre-colored cows with white rumps, picking
the ears and tying them in bundles or planting the tiny
plants with great rapidity. Of about equal area to these
paddy fields, which are stepped up hill and down dale,
are the vast kampongs where each family lives surrounded by an earth wall with an ornate doorway amidst
a mass of little hutlike shrines, raised seats, and images.
These walls are a great feature of the countryside. Some
are of neat native bricks, and all are covered with a little
roof to prevent damage by rain.

We followed the coast road for some way to the west
and then turned inland, crossing a mass of low hills covered to their tops with paddy fields, stopping several
times to inspect the Hindu temples. These are walled-in
clearings with a vast gateway of brick with very elaborate
Balinese carvings, mostly of a cock's-comb shape, in

stone, let in, and numerous carved stone images of gods with grotesque faces. Inside there is at least one tall, elaborately carved shrine, square and enclosed with four double doors of gold and colored work in bas-relief. Innumerable little roofed, pillarlike shrines stand around, some having figures of gods, others empty seats, still others a platform for little offerings. The Balinese are all Hindus but take little interest in religion beyond feasts, holidays, and gods in "silver, wood and brass." I asked the little boys and men who came into the temples the names of the various images, but all they said was, "It is a god."

Finally we descended to the plain and arrived at Denpasar. After a rest I had my driver take me on to Kloengkoeng, which lies east of Denpasar. Here there is a "sacred forest." This was (then at least) a large wood of really vast trees, completely clear of any vegetation below, but instead carpeted with vivid green moss. There were millions of cicadas, the buzzing and rasping of which was almost deafening; and there were also crowds of gray Crab-eating Macaques (*Cynamolgus irus*), to whom in fact the wood belonged. These monkeys are held in great reverence in Bali and are never molested. In this wood they apparently subsisted mainly on bowls of rice and other delicacies placed just inside the wood by the local residents. There is a temple in the midst of this forest, and I was escorted there by an old man who seemed to have some sort of official status, though I could not make out what it was. I returned to this wood on several occasions, taking handfuls of corn or fruit to feed to the macaques who crowded round. As I left one evening I met the old man who had first escorted me, and he proceeded to berate me in no uncertain terms, though I could not make out a single word. He seemed to realize this and indicated that I should accompany him forthwith. I followed meekly, wondering all the while what I might have done to offend the sacred monkeys and what the penalties might be. Ushered into the local equivalent of a chamber of commerce, my transgressions were explained to the man in charge—an enormous Hollander—who promptly spluttered and then informed me that I must either stay out of the forest or leave town. They were not in the least worried about the monkeys; it was my stupidity that alarmed them. The Macaques are among the ruffians of the monkey world and can be most frightfully dangerous. I had, in my innocence, exposed myself to attack and, at the very least, serious injury at the hands of these "enlightened ones."

The Crab-eating Macaques seldom live far from the sea or fresh water, and the majority inhabit coastal mangrove swamps where there is almost nothing of a vegetable nature to eat, few insects (except mosquitoes, generally counted by billions), but plenty of crustaceans. However, they do relish fruit and grains and on many islands do considerable damage to crops, raiding gardens and plantations and generally behaving like a bunch of juvenile delinquents. One wonders whether the Balinese custom of allocating them property of their own and feeding them may have originated in self-defense.

The rock tombs of the rajahs are also at Kloengkoeng, and I was taken to see these. All were most interesting, as were their surroundings. There were wonderful baths where crystal-clear water lay in an ornate pond and flowed down through gorgeous mouths and other spouts into other shallow pools. The tombs themselves are all artificial caves, perfectly ventilated by sheltered chimneys, and cover a large area. After inspecting these, I was taken on to another site where, behind the usual shrines, there were two pagodas and, at the back of the clearing in which they stood, a cave with a floor gradually sloping up to the roof. The whole of this cave from its mouth to its farthest recesses was obscured absolutely, literally, and entirely by a seething, squeaking mass of large gray leaf-nosed bats.* The air was thick with them on the wing, every inch of the roof covered and the floor inches deep in black droppings. The smell was peculiar to bats and was quite overwhelming, but I was so fascinated that I watched for nearly an hour. They disliked the smoke from my cigarette, and when it reached the roof, the bats in that immediate area all decamped, swirling around in the cave to find an unpolluted spot.

From a beach of fine gray sand just across the road from the bat cave I could see the blue-gray hills of Lombok through the haze. It was the closest I got to that island, though I was not too disappointed, since it is not a collector's paradise.

Having seen most of what there was to see near Denpasar, I once more packed up my things and left in the car for Kintamani where I was to have lunch. We drove for about an hour, evidently ascending some 5,900 feet which I never noticed. The walled kampongs gave way to ordinary *atap* houses, and the vegetation first became

---

*What species of bat this was I do not know. The Leaf-nosed Bats are all New World species, but a number of Oriental species do have fleshy appendages about the mouth and nose and can legitimately be described as "leaf-nosed." [S. W. S.]

English and then typically Scottish. Suddenly we arrived at the edge of a perfectly vast crater, in which on the right at the foot of the highest point lay a long curved lake and in the center rose a huge cone of lava and ash with two large vents, smoking slightly around their rims with blue and white vapors. At the foot of this and to the left lay a sea of recently emitted yet black ash, smoking here and there. We drove to the left around this crater to the Kintamani rest house, through a desolate, dirty, straggling village built on wasteland. Having looked at this place and felt the cold and seen the general likeness to Scotland, I announced that I was ready to leave. However, the manager of the rest house was adamant that I should take at least a short walk with him, as he had something very curious to show me. His expression was so odd that I was intrigued despite the cold and consented to follow him.

Now, when I was a really little nipper I spent quite a bit of time on my godfather's steam yachts (actually, he had a series of them)* and on one trip we visited the Songe Fjord in Norway. I was permitted to go ashore to chumble about pretty much as I wished, though McKelvie kept an eye on me and on one occasion took me up a valley that led into the fjord. Here there seemed to be something wrong with gravity: there were innumerable pebbles lying about, but they gave the impression of "floating" a miniscule distance off the ground, and of not being at all soundly "attached" to it. I know this

---

*Ivan's godfather was James McKelvie, a coal exporter. His yachts (in chronological order) were the *Melisande*, *Gladys*, and *Surf*, and were enormous. [S. W. S.]

sounds balmy, but I can think of no other way to describe it. And this same phenomenon was evident in the crater at Kintamani. So far as I know, these are the only two places where this occurs, no one knows why or how; but I am afraid I disappointed my guide, who naturally expected more of a reaction on my part. He was only somewhat mollified by the acquisition of new information on "floating" pebbles.

Returning to the car we started on again. We climbed for a bit and then began the descent by a beautiful banked and twisting road. We became enveloped in mist and I sank beneath my burberry. At last we got down into the lovely warm plain again, through a huge and very neat village where my driver managed to kill first a dog and then a tiny pig. Admittedly, both wander freely through the streets, but my driver displayed all the symptoms of advanced lunacy typical of motorists in that part of the world. It must be the climate.

Arriving back in Singaradja (for which Boeleleng is the port), I drove to Phatima's house. She was not in, but I was received by the most beautiful Balinese girl I ever saw anywhere. Alas, Phatima soon arrived, but she greeted me as an old friend and, taking me into her bedroom, displayed all her wares: silver earrings, golden-threaded sarongs, and carved gods. I bought a lovely gold ring for my mother—not buying something was not allowed—and Phatima then served excellent coffee and cigarettes. Afterward she drove with me to the rest house. It was now raining like hell, and we covered ourselves with my burberry, and she put on my topee. She saw me comfortably settled in my room, then left after taking a tender farewell.

Later that evening I rounded up Achi to make certain that he was clear about my plans for the next day. He looked very slightly dubious but had the details down pat. Nona greeted me enthusiastically, but I left her with Achi, being uncertain of her reception at the rest house. She had certainly recovered from her sea sickness, and I felt rather bad about what I had in store for her, but Achi said he would cope. Had I known what he had in mind I would have been spared some mental anguish, but his method eliminated argument and I retired to bed to dream of Macassar—the name that had always spelt tropics to me.

❧ 10 ❧

By Prau to Celebes: Sea-snakes and Storms

THE SUN HAD RISEN BUT WAS still blanketed by the whitish muffle that joins sea to sky. I waited upon the beach in Bali, seated upon a pile of cases, watching the sea-going praus. Among these was the sturdy vessel that I had already inspected some time before at a small port on the coast of Java. The eyes painted on either side of the prow of this vessel held a sad and woebegone expression. But on board, several small brown men were extremely busy. I hailed them, and they waved back cheerily. The car that had brought me to the beach with my possessions at dawn had long since departed; but Achi, for some unfathomable reason, had not yet turned up, with the box that contained all my personal belongings and civilized clothes. We waited two hours more, and then I decided to abandon both Achi and my clothes rather than miss the trip.

The principal reason for my choosing to travel by native prau to Celebes when small yachtlike passenger boats made the trip upon regular schedule was that I wanted to collect sea-snakes. I have mentioned seeing great numbers of these in the Malacca Straits, but, of course, one cannot collect them while traveling on a swift passenger vessel running on a schedule. They are of considerable interest to science, not having been so extensively collected as land snakes.

At eleven o'clock, therefore, we let go the communally owned shoreline, waved to the busy occupants of the other praus, hoisted two oddly shaped sails—the larger of canvas, the small one aft of split bamboo—and pushed off.

The prau was a very large one, with an immense pan-shaped central well deck filled to the lip of the bulwarks with native merchandise. There were bales of dried fish, dried sea slugs on the way to the Chinese markets, dried fruits, bundles of goat hides, and an endless assortment of bales, bundles, and rough crates bulging with undefinable produce. All these were neatly bedded down so that they formed a more or less level false deck flush with the edge of the vessel; and over them was spread a gigantic net constructed of pieces of rope, sharks' hide, and creeper ropes. This was pegged into slots on the gunwale and upon it mats, rough tarpaulins, and countless batik sarongs were stretched.

The two extremities of the boat were really small triangular floating houses, with three stories for'ard and four aft. They were constructed with watertight bulkheads facing the well deck, which was nothing more than two great sides like those of a dinghy; these sides connected the two floating "houses." The reason for all this is not obvious and was quite unknown to me at the time.

Everybody lived upon the cargo amidships, the poops being filled with a mixture of ship's supplies like a chandler's warehouse, children in batik cribs, more dried fish, privately owned rice, and spaces covered with old pieces of corrugated iron upon which food was always cooking. I never learned the extent of the ship's company, for there were always more people asleep than awake, the children appeared to be interchangeable, and several of the women were more or less troglodytic, appearing only after dark. Superb seamanship and accurate navigation appeared to be the keynote of the vessel's progress, but I saw no instruments aboard, not even a compass; and yet we made a passage of approximately eighty miles across the angry and treacherous Java Sea.

The first day and night were uneventful. No sea-snakes appeared, but it was delightful to lie under a mat parasol clad in a sarong, with one's bare feet stuck over the gunwale to catch the cool draft created by the vessel's progress. The night was even more perfect. Nowhere in the world is the moon brighter or the stars more vivid than around the Java Sea.

The initial period of delightful laziness, however, gave way to one of intense activity. Sea-snakes became numerous, and many of the men as well as the captain became enthusiastic. Various methods of capture were suggested —hook and line, nooses, nets, and other less probable devices. The captain plumped for nets, of which he carried an abundance; and since I was unable to enter the argument and nobody had ever attempted to catch the creatures before, he won his point. Sail was dropped, and we drifted with great nets trailing in all directions. We caught innumerable fish and a small dolphin and saw sea-snakes on both sides of the net, but caught none. It was while I was occupied with the dolphin that a small boy caught a snake from the bows with a circular Chinese casting net. Excitement ran high, and the reptile was belabored. It promptly disappeared down a deep crevice between the cargo and did not re-emerge. This was considered to be the will of Allah, which it probably was, and so it remained there.

Operations recommenced, and went on for hours with but little abatement of enthusiasm. I think everybody enjoyed the novelty of the game. We then plowed on through an area devoid of snakes and subsequently came upon another patch of brilliant red-and-black ones, and the process was repeated. The captain proved himself the man of the hour by landing and killing four of the snakes. We were much elated, and he decided to wallow in the placid swell during the whole night, so that we might have a chance the next day. My agreement with him included an extra bonus for snakes caught during the voyage.

That evening a general holiday was declared; small oil lamps were lit—a thing that had not previously been done; and after a communal meal, small bamboo xylophones and tiny shell pipes were brought out, and soft, melodious, liquid chants spread over the oily, heaving waters.

Everything was so soothing that when my work was completed on the day's catches, I fell asleep on the after poop. When I awoke, it was pitch-dark, and there was a great commotion going on below. Groping in the dark, I found the rough companionway of bamboo poles and descended to the well; somebody ran into me headlong, and I bawled at them to find out what was afoot, but nobody replied. The sound of the big sail being hoisted came to me, and I made my way forward to interrogate some of the men. There was a slight drizzle falling. The sound of hammering came from both fore and aft, and the air seemed to be filled with a strange, indefinable wailing noise. I reached the men and painstakingly put my questions in my best Malay. For answer I was shouted at in Buginese, Salayanese, and sundry other languages, and so retired beaten to the after poop where I kept my possessions to search for a flashlight. When I reached the bulkhead and groped along toward the door, I bumped into more people and, making a plunge for the door, ran headlong into solid wood. Nursing my nose, I groped around. To my astonishment I found that the door had been completely boarded up with thick planks. I was dumbfounded. Then I was hailed.

"Tuan Inggris, Tuan Inggris!" the captain's voice rang out of the darkness and the hubbub.

I found him on the after poop.

"What's the matter?" I inquired.

But all I heard was the oft-repeated and greatly emphasized word *laut,* which means "sea," and something else that sounded like "angry bazaar." I learned later what *that* meant, but I did immediately begin to grasp the significance of the company's behavior, for the ship was now heaving noticeably. I still wanted my flashlight and so asked the captain how I could get at it. For answer he

/ *133*

half dragged, half pushed me down a small hatchway into the stuffy interior of the poop.

Here a hurricane lamp burned, and by its light I descried the captain's family and several others, huddled together in a corner, looking somewhat scared. I unearthed my torch and returned to the little deck above. Men were working like demons, lashing the big sail fore and aft with endless additional ropes and thongs. Rain was now descending in a solid cascade, and a slight warm breeze had sprung up. I clung to the heaving rail and watched proceedings, shining my flashlight beam here and there. The captain had disappeared.

Then it happened: More abruptly than one could have believed possible, and without previous warning of any kind, the rain falling through the beam of light turned suddenly at right angles, and a wind hit me from the port beam with a force that took my breath away. The great lumbering prau heeled over like a wallowing sea-monster, shipping a waterfall of inky water to starboard. She remained over at a dizzy angle, and during this interlude everybody scrambled onto the poops. By the time the sail had pulled the head of the vessel into the wind, and she had therefore righted herself, everybody except myself and the captain was below. Stupidly protesting, I was pulled below also.

As my head sank through the little hatchway, a jet of solid salt water hit me in the face, smashing my head against the frame. I slithered down the companionway and remembered no more for some hours, though my insensibility merged into a deep and fretful sleep. When I came fully around, with a lump on my head and a splitting headache, it was undeniably ten o'clock in the morning; and yet the small cabin was in total darkness but for the flickering and madly swinging lamp. The world was filled with an endless roaring, and my body rose and fell and rolled about so that I expected it to leave the hard deck at any moment. Around me, the company gripped each other and any stable object, bracing themselves with their toes against the timbers.

The presentation of a highly valued tin of tobacco to the captain won me the (really very dubious) privilege of going above.

The first fury of the storm had passed by. What was left was half a gale and a sea churned up like whipped cream. Damp clouds raced across the sky, which had dropped to a few hundred feet above the mast; sharp-pointed peaks of foam danced upon an immense, steep swell. But the most amazing thing was that we were awash.

Instead of two feet of freeboard, we now had some six inches; water stood at the same level both within and without the gunwales. The greedy sea gurgled up and down between the bales of merchandise and slopped in and out of the vessel as it wished. I was nearly an hour absorbing this fact as I stood incredulously watching the bales of dried fish and fruits, now swollen and soggy, rising and falling beneath the great net.

At sundown the wind vanished suddenly and the dark clouds rolled away, leaving a trail of thin white mist that hurried after them. A golden sun blazed out, illuminating an exalted sky, puffed with billowing white clouds. The crew began to appear.

Modern pumps in excellent condition, which I had not seen before, were uncovered; and for hours and hours seawater was spouted back into its own environment, and the vessel presumably rose gently—though the result, when the pumps began to gurgle far below, was not very noticeable, for the cargo was saturated and now extraordinarily heavy. An amazing medley of objects were raised aloft on lines to dry, the mats came out again, and acrid smoke belched from the poops once more.

It was not until the next morning when I came to look for my notebook that I realized that I had left my precious snakes in the corner of the well deck where I had worked. I ran to look for them. They had gone overboard, with every other movable object.

The captain was as sympathetic as I could wish and offered to return to the place where we had caught them. I looked at him in amazement; did he know where that spot had been, after running before the storm and its aftermath for twelve hours? I asked him if he knew where we were.

He looked overboard at the sea; then he scanned the sky and replied simply, *"Mowou"* or, "Yes." And he did know, because a day later we entered the port of Macassar, the place to which he had guaranteed to take me.

Bidding my friends farewell, I ascended the steep stone steps to the pier, feeling very gloomy indeed, for I had lost most of my few possessions and failed to gain my precious sea-snakes—I could not accept the captain's generous offer because of the limited time I had for this "side trip." Having dealt with the customs authorities, I went on through a customs warehouse. As I emerged into the sunlight, I was greeted by a shout.

"Tuan, *Tuan!*"

I swung round, and there stood Achi. Beside him was my trunk. I later discovered that he had left by the mail boat at his own expense at dawn on the day of my departure from Bali, though he remained extremely vague about *why* he had done so.

It was some time later that I thought to ask him about the "angry bazaar." Since I threw this question at him a propos of absolutely nothing, his reply was somewhat delayed, but finally comprehension dawned on his face and he said, "Oh, Tuan; you mean *angin besar.* This means big wind."

❧ 11 ❧

---

*Celebes: Babirusa, and How Not to
Catch Rats*

IT WAS A LOVELY DAY, AND
the old town lying behind the mile of straight wharf was
just as I expected it to be. It was originally a Portuguese
settlement, and there were still signs of their occupation.
Four or five long streets ran parallel to the sea, narrow
and flanked by Chinese, Arab, native, and Indian shops.
The natives here were not beautiful, being darker
skinned and differently dressed from those I had met
before. Too, these people seemed to age much younger
than the other Malay peoples, for old women were preva-
lent and all the muscular men had shriveled old faces.

I was very keen to do some collecting here, for I had
now crossed Wallace's Line. This line is shown on the
map [Figure 1] of the East Indies [Indonesia] and must
look purely arbitrary and even a bit balmy to the non-

GREEN SILENCE

zoologist, running as it does between Bali and Lombok, which are only a few miles apart. In fact, it marks a distinct boundary between Asiatic and Australopapuan fauna. Animals found on one side of the Line simply are not found on the other. True, there are, as I have pointed out before, animals that are found on only one or a few islands, but these are never found on both sides of Wallace's Line. Exactly why this should be, no one knows. The distances between many of the islands are small, and often the sea is shallow, so that this should not in itself constitute a barrier to animal "emigration" and, of course, would not affect bird populations, though these are equally distinct.

Leaving Achi in charge of my baggage and of Nona, I went off to see the British Consul, to whom I explained the object of my travels and showed my British Museum letter. At this latter, he sat up and began telephoning, saying I was from the Government and my wants must be seen to immediately. He also gave me a letter of introduction to the manager of a rubber and coffee plantation far in the interior of the southwest peninsula, with instructions on how I should travel there. I then returned to the wharf where Achi and I sorted out the things we should need, leaving the heavy luggage in the customs building, since it would be impossible to carry it all with us, and found—after considerable effort—a couple of chaps to cart our luggage to the hotel where I proposed to spend the night. It was not the best of hotels, even for remote Southeast Asia, and the rooms were sort of ghastly, bare loose-boxes, but it did have its compensations.

Having been told that an Australian who had been

catching live birds in Papua was staying at the hotel while waiting for a boat for Europe, I asked at the hotel but, not then knowing his name and the clerk only guessing whom I wanted, I found myself in a room with the wrong man, who had neither clothes nor false teeth to hand. I retired as gracefully as possible to wait on the verandah, and Meyer, in fact a German who had lived most of his life in England, soon returned and readily agreed to show me his small but superb collection of Birds of Paradise, lories, kingfishers, etc. He had four of the rare and beautiful Wallace's Standard Wing (*Semioptera wallacii*), somewhat mouse colored, with a bronzy back and a violet head, green edges to the pectoral feathers, and a kind of green shield that extends from the fore-neck back, in tufts, to the flanks, and two long narrow white plumes at the bend of each wing; as well as several Twelve-wired Birds of Paradise (*Seleucides ignotus*), which are iridescent black, with emerald edges on the breast plumes and lemon-yellow sides and belly. Oddly enough, these beautiful birds are related to the Crows. I had a long talk with Meyer about my proposed plans, and he was most helpful.

Thus it was that I leapt out of bed at seven thirty the next morning and packed, dressed, and ordered breakfast all at the same time. At eight thirty I and my "entourage" were loaded into a magnificent Packard and whisked to what passed for a bus depot. The bus arrived after a time. It was old and divided into three compartments, i.e., the driving seat, with two first-class places beside it; a wire cage for the mail bags, in which—going by post—was a little dusky beauty covered in the most lovely jewelry and clothed in beautifully colored silks;

and a third, wired-in on three sides with facing seats for native passengers. The bus had a crew of four: a driver, two boys, and a very nice, cheery Malay foreman in a pink suit who was told to see that I was comfortable, being informed that I was from the British Government and well known to the Consul. The Malay and I climbed up by the driver, and we set off on our eight-hour run. All the way we kept stopping to pick up passengers with baskets of durians or other fruits, bargaining with them for the fare; if, however, they did not get their price, they simply refused to come. It was not a very comfortable ride, since we rattled along at terrific speed and the seat was very narrow and, for me at least, the leg space practically nil.

We arrived at last, but there was no one to meet me and no known way to get to the estate, so we made do with the rather primitive facilities at the rest house, and the next morning not one but two cars showed up to convey us to our destination. The drive was along a very good road planted with an avenue of trees and crossing rivers and streams by very fine steel bridges, all of which seemed very much out of keeping with the wild, unpopulated country and tropical vegetation.

My host's bungalow was a large, well-appointed wooden structure, then in the course of being painted, and my room was comfortable but not very efficient since there were no cupboards, pegs, or shelves in or on which to stow my things. Nevertheless, I managed to arrange my clothes and collecting gear in some semblance of order, a situation which did not last, of course; everything was soon covered in mold and little white toadstools!

Over an enormous rijsttafel I met the manager's wife and two children—and a pretty little half-caste girl who was probably his daughter, though I did not ask—and his mother, a very sweet old lady who did everything possible to make me feel at home. Afterward we had *pisangs* [bananas] and durians. These latter were exceptionally good, being almost all a huge brown stone covered with a stringy white soft substance with a unique flavor. I was warned that eating too many encourages ulcers and can only wonder about the native population; the small mountains of durian stones that one sees beside each *atap* hut would seem to indicate a thoroughly ulcerated citizenry.

The next morning I was wakened at 5:15 A.M., but got up to breakfast at six o'clock. I found my host waiting for me, so we started right away on two vast and rather good plates of porridge, followed by currant bread and cheese and fruit. We then sat about and smoked, for it was raining (as usual). After a bit he went off to the "garden," as he called it, and I decided I had best get down to work.

Achi was turned on to making a bamboo stake for each rat trap while I went along to the "factory" to get string. It began to pour again, and I took shelter in several buildings before I got to the sending-off shed where I waited for the assistant, a man I had met the day before, but he was not helpful. At last a Chinese worker got me a mass of it, which we all unraveled while waiting for the rain to stop. Returning to the house, I began getting the strings onto the traps, assisted by a gardener and his boy and Achi. At about four o'clock Achi and I set out for the boundary of the estate, and I was delighted to see real virgin jungle, which we entered by a rudimentary path made by wood cutters.

Crossing a tiny river, we laid a line of twenty-six traps, running from it straight up the hill into the jungle. The whole hill was of soft clay, it was raining, and every other tree was a mass of vast thorns, while nearly all the leaves had a cutting edge. Masses of large black ants seemed to resent our intrusion into their domains and retaliated by inflicting wasplike bites. Achi baited the traps, tied on the stakes, and set them, while I ran into the jungle and laid them. The line was a long one, and Achi had to move three times; it was nearly dark by the time we got back.

The next morning I dressed quickly—an easy thing, since rubber shoes, trousers, and an Airtex vest were all that was required—and went off with Achi to look at my traps. It was very wet, and after a lot of slipping about on the hopelessly muddy slope, I found that there was absolutely nothing in them, although nearly all the *klapa* (coconut) had been nibbled. So, taking up all the traps, we waded along the stream, since it was the only way of moving in this dense, thorn-clad forest, and relaid them with great care up the hill further to the right, taking six traps away with us. It was raining hard as we got back, so I got into pyjamas and wrote in my diary until lunch.

After lunch, taking only insect-collecting things, we went down to another river on the other side of the estate, bordered by tall *lallong*, and as the sun was now shining very brightly, I expected to find many bugs, but there were none to speak of. Walking was very difficult, and after a bit we returned home, and I skinned a peculiar little short-tailed gray shrew that had been caught in one of the traps I had given Achi to set in the kampong.

This came out very well, and although Achi was most attentive, he complained of *sakit kepala* (a headache), whereupon I dosed him with aspirin. In a few minutes he was better, and we went again to the traps, but still there was nothing. So we swung them around, putting them parallel to the river. I baited and set them while he laid them. This latter is tedious work as only two can be carried set at a time. I then took others we had brought out with us and laid them in another part of the jungle about a mile to the left on the near bank.

The next morning, as usual, there was nothing in the traps though the baits had been thoroughly nibbled. Sitting down to examine the situation, I discovered the reason for the failure: the traps were extremely bad in that they required much movement of the bait to spring them. After rebaiting we moved on to the smaller line, in the last one of which, to my great delight, I found a very fine rat. It was silvery gray above and white tinged with pink beneath, the feet and legs gray above and pink beneath, and the underside of the toes oddly ridged. The tail was dark gray on the upper half and pure white on the "end half." When I picked the trap up, there was a distinct rustling sound, and then I saw that the trap was a mass of huge black ants which were fast swarming onto my arm. As they began to bite, Achi and I started "squashing them off." Then, putting the whole trap in the butterfly net, I slid almost the whole way to the bottom of the hill in my excitement, where I released the rat and then relaid the trap down by the stream. We then returned to the house where I skinned the rat, and Achi went off to look for butterflies, returning with quite a good collection.

After lunch we charged off into the jungle again to inspect the long line of traps, which I intended re-laying elsewhere. I sent Achi to collect the traps while I waited in the stream. From here I could catch the murmuring, moaning sounds made by wild pigs, or Babirusa [see Figure 21], moving about in the swamps nearby. These animals are found only in the island of Celebes and a few small neighboring islands such as Boeroe. They are denizens of the damp forests and stay by rivers and other water, in which they love to bathe and swim; in fact, they customarily enter the water for pleasure and on occasion swim in the sea to reach small islands off the coast or to cross lagoons and estuaries, even though many of those places are full of sharks.

They are lightly built animals and swift runners. The skin is earth colored, dry, rough, and altogether like bark, though it hangs in loose folds. The tail is short and has no tuft at the end. Indeed, they are almost hairless, except along the crest of the high, arched back, where there are a few coarse hairs. The females have small tusks, while those of the male are ridiculous devices for which there appears to be no satisfactory explanation. All teeth and most tusks have a hard, white, shiny outside surface of enamel, but the tusks of Babirusas have no enamel at all and go on growing all the time. And the tusks are so long that the upper ones, which may be more than a foot long, circle over backward above the eyes, then turn downward and actually touch the top of the muzzle, and finally, in old males, go forward again, forming complete circles. Even the lower tusks, or tushes, curve upward and backward to a great length. Sometimes when a rabbit or rat meets with an accident to its lower front teeth, the upper ones (which go on growing all the time) get longer and longer because they have nothing to grind against. Thus, in exceptional cases, these animals may be killed by their own front teeth growing back into their mouths, upward into the back of their palates, and, eventually, right through their heads, coming out on the top. In the case of the rat or the rabbit this circular growth is abnormal and lethal, but with the Babirusa the same sort of thing is quite natural, and the upper tusks never go into the mouth at all, their direction of growth being outward.

Some of the attempts to explain why they have these peculiar teeth are even more ridiculous than the teeth themselves. Some people actually suggested that the Babirusas hang themselves up on branches, using the tusks as hooks, when tired or when their necks ache from stooping so much to feed on the ground. What happens to the poor wretched females and babies who don't have great hooked tusks nobody has explained. Other suggestions have been no more helpful than this one, but one must assume that they have some purpose, though I have no idea what it might be.

Babirusas cling together in small herds and betray their whereabouts by grunting like pigs and giving vent to endless low moans like wild boars, which is a noise that one would never attribute to a pig unless one knew about it. The herds are on the move at night, as the animals feed only after dark, though I have seen them basking in full sunlight during the day. Admittedly they were then all either half or fully asleep. The young are very small and rather helpless and, unlike the young of most pigs, are not striped and have rather more hair than their elders. Usually they have only one baby at a time, two apparently constituting a large family.

The people of Celebes hunt Babirusas for food but I found the meat about as tasty as a brown paper bag.*

Still engrossed in the murmurings of the Babirusas, I was jolted somewhat by Achi's sudden arrival with another, larger specimen of the same rat caught that morning. We then inspected and rebaited the other lot of traps; finding nothing in them, we laid a fresh line right up the opposite side of the ravine, mostly at the mouths of fresh holes. After dinner I hauled my table out into the living room under the light and did not retire until I had sewn up the rat. It was a rather smelly job, since decomposition had distinctly set in about the stomach, and rubber gloves had to be worn. Alas, when finished it looked very much like "a drowned rat in a thunderstorm."

The next morning I could not drag myself out of bed until six thirty, and then I had breakfast and sat about in my pyjamas for some time, feeling far from well and rather undecided as to whether a visit to the traps should be personal. However, the thought of Alfred Russel Wallace's various ailments and ultimate success urged me forward and after dressing, I proceeded with Achi in tow. As we descended into the jungle I felt distinctly worse, and a headache crept slowly over my eyes. Slow progression soon remedied this latter, but the sight of twenty-eight entirely unsprung traps in apparently ideal posi-

---

*An editor once rewrote Ivan's comment on this to indicate that "They are very good to eat." I asked Ivan about this; his reply was and is unprintable. [S. W. S.]

tion added depression and gloom to my condition. Having rebaited, we moved slowly about, taking a few insects. The virgin jungle is to my mind one of the most wonderful sights imaginable; it is a world all its own, apart from *Homo sapiens* but absolutely complete in itself. The weird calls of birds echoing from narrow valley to narrow valley, the crash of falling fruits, the continuous "scissor-grinding," buzzing, and "circular-saw" noises of innumerable cicadas that are always out of reach, the incessant drip of vast bulbs of water (I can call them nothing else), seem only to intensify the otherwise deathly, motionless silence. The gigantic smooth-trunked trees topped by a billowing mass of rather shiny dark-green foliage make a mysterious covering to the tangled mass of exotic palms, tree-ferns, and curious-shaped leaves that lie still in the dusk beneath, while here and there the branches of the tall trees are shaken intermittently by a troop of jet-black monkeys, or the air is rent by the screaming of a flight of lories.*

On returning to the house, I felt very bad indeed and, sending Achi off to "collect bugs," I fell into bed and slept until noon. After lunch I sat about for a bit and put a lot of butterflies into papers before setting out for a stroll around with the bug nets. I chased a very fine *Papilio* butterfly around the house, which produced screams of joy from the natives in the next house and our boys and made the crowd of coolies going to work stop and gaze open-mouthed. Four little naked boys of varying ages were following us around, catching in their hands things that I could not get near with my net. One

---

*A type of parrot.

boy suddenly began to howl and was only comforted by the vision of me up to the knees in a concealed drain of dirty stinking water from the factory. Going into a clearing between the estate and the big river, we began searching among some solitary banana trees for *binatang binatang,** when with a scream the smallest boy pointed out a large, fat-bodied, pale-green praying mantis viewing the world through its absurdly prominent eyes from the very tip of a dead branch. This was secured after a fine display of "movements of fright" by both parties. A little further on we were startled by the vision of a fast-retreating jet-black, six-foot snake, which I chased with the butterfly net, which I bent double in my attempts to get it over the snake's head. With large bamboos that were lying around everywhere we tried to get it out into the open from a clump of small bushes, but it had wisely retreated into the *lallong.*

This was enough, so I thought, for one day and I retreated to the house, only to find that Achi had procured another of the peculiar little gray shrews. So I settled down to skin this, much to the interest of the Chinese carpenters who had arrived to build a new verandah, a tremendous amount of which they had completed with astounding energy during the course of the day. The shrew was very small and particularly interesting, being a female. The teats, eight in number, run from the anus diagonally up each of the hind legs on the inside, while on the middle of the back is a drawn-out hexagon of very short fine hairs. There was much milk

---

*"Animals." Kitchen Malay produces plurals and comparative adjectives by repeating the word.

in the mammary glands, which smelled very sweet, but I managed the skinning without too much trouble.

After dinner my host put me through a kind of medical third degree, announced that my complaint was malaria, and accordingly dosed me with foul-tasting quinine. I retired to bed, planning to stay there indefinitely.

At six o'clock I was awakened by yells from my host announcing that Achi had arrived with two interesting rats from the jungle traps. Rushing out, I found him just arriving, and I delved into the bag he was carrying, which contained, among the mass of bottles, coconut, and forceps, two very fine rats—one large, much like the common *Ratus norwegicus* but having an orange underside, and the other a very small gray rat, tinged with gold above and pale buff beneath. I breakfasted in a cheery frame of mind, thinking work had really begun. The Chinese carpenters had arrived to finish the verandah, and from one of them I bought a very fine little file. We then set off for the jungle and the long line of traps. Here I spent some two hours filing the traps at the critical point and greasing them so that they were easily sprung. I then sent Achi off to grease and file the others while I returned to the house to skin the rats.

I was in the midst of this when Achi turned up in a state of great excitement, saying he had seen an *ular besar besar* (tremendous snake) about twenty-three feet long. He had been bending over one of the traps and, looking up, saw the snake crossing from one tree to another. Borrowing my host's gun, I proceeded to the jungle, with Achi carrying all collecting equipment. Achi dived into the jungle above the first small line of traps and after a bit pointed at a place where two quite thin creeper-covered trees arched over a patch of beaten-down thicket and explained at great length where the *ular* had been. We spent nearly half an hour combing the area but saw no sign of the snake. Our luck in general was not good. I caught in the net a weird frog with iridescent emerald-green patches on its head, but it escaped during transference to the killing bottle by a wild leap onto Achi's chest and a subsequent series of leaps that proved beyond doubt that it was far more agile than the two of us together. The traps, of course, were all empty, and we returned to the house feeling somewhat dismal. Adding insult to injury, on our arrival the houseboy came rushing up to me and showed me a lovely gold and yellow tree snake at the end of a stick, three little rats in a hollow bamboo, and a large reddish rat alive in a kerosene tin, tied by the hind leg to a piece of bamboo, which the natives had brought me.

I skinned the large rat and was about to start on the others—I had not taken the snake, because, like all the others they brought, it had been chopped almost in half in the middle—when my host hauled me off to dinner, insisting that I come since guests had arrived. He also insisted that I first do something about my appearance. After a week in the jungle, living in the house in pyjamas and in the jungle in wet, muddy trousers, vest, and rubber shoes, without vaseline or hair oil, with no basin or looking glass to shave with, and bitten regularly on the face by bugs of every kind, one does not look very pretty. Thus it was that after half an hour cleaning, shaving with difficulty by lamplight over a basin on a chair, and soaping my now long hair to make it lie down, I was still only barely respectable. In the rather dim light in the house

I passed muster but made my escape as soon as I could.

The next day was the "free day" of the month, and consequently we did not get up till eight thirty, when I found my host in superb white clothing, a great contrast to his khaki working shorts and shirt. I could not finish breakfast, as I suddenly felt violently sick. After a cigarette I donned rubber gloves, as I had several small cuts on my hands and the area beneath my left thumbnail was becoming very sore, and finished skinning the rats. Then, putting on my old rags, I virtuously proceeded alone to the jungle—Achi having gone off to celebrate the *hari besar* (big day or holiday)—expecting to find a rat in every trap. I caught some interesting *Hymenoptera* [ants, bees, wasps, and certain flies] on the way, and after crawling to the traps with difficulty, I found not one even sprung! It was a sunny day, and as I traversed the jungle clearings wonderful *Papilios* flitted around out of reach, hundreds of gorgeous-colored lizards disappeared at sight or glided from tree to tree far above me, and much desired Longicorns went, as if flicked, from the fallen tree trunks. Hard and long I tried to catch even one of these, but all in vain. Thus it was two thirty before I got back to the house weary and very disappointed and in fact sick and shaky, my left thumb burning and throbbing terribly. I burnt my surgical scalpel and, after cutting down my nail, made an incision into the quick, washed it in strong permanganate-of-potash solution, and bound it up with a wet dressing of boracic lint. My host had a look at it and said that if it were not better by morning, I should return to Macassar to see a doctor there. He was going to Boeloekoemba himself but would take me on to Bonthein (60 kilometers beyond [about 37 miles]), where I could certainly find transport to Macassar.

Accordingly I spent the next morning sorting and packing the insects while Achi made a dash to collect all the traps—no rats of course!—and was ready roughly by the time my host's very efficient Chinese chauffeur (in plush cap and superlative raincoat) came to collect me and my luggage. After what seemed like an eternity Achi and I were deposited with our somewhat peculiar pile of belongings, with Nona perched on top, in Bonthein, where the blithe predictions of transport appeared somewhat overoptimistic. Achi, as usual, came to my rescue; having spotted an empty bus, he proceeded to produce the driver and crew. We attempted to reduce the cost (really not very great in any case) by going off through the streets yelling "Macassar Macassar pigi Macassar" but no one seemed inclined to visit that vast metropolis, so off we went at breakneck speed. Once we stopped to tie some part of the auto's mechanism on with rope, and again at a little town after it was dark, where with great difficulty I was made to understand that they wanted to take on five vast bags of corn as ballast, as one of the crew, a little man in huge gray Oxford bags [trousers] was getting complications in the "solar plexus" from the easy motion. The bags of corn were carried out by meager lamplight from a house built on piles over the water, and, of course, one of the men went straight through the rotten boards of the little bridge to the roadway under the weight of his load. We then proceeded in a far more comfortable manner but at no less speed.

Once installed at the hotel in Macassar, I got the manager to ring up the doctor and put me into a taxi for his house. He examined my thumb and said I had done right and that it was very healthy; he also told me that I had not got malaria but was rather low from strenuous exercise in the jungle. I returned to the hotel, had a good dinner, and went straight to bed.

The next morning, bolstered by the good doctor's diagnoses and some powders of a pick-me-up nature, I conferred with Achi, and we once again sorted our belongings, parking still more boxes and bundles at the customs house, and headed for the nearest patch of virgin jungle—where we proceeded to get thoroughly lost and Achi taught me to draw.

❧ 12 ❧

A Digression: How to Draw Animals

I SHOULD LIKE TO DIGRESS here to answer a question I have often been asked: How do you draw animals? And how did you learn to do so?

Depicting animals is more closely akin to depicting the human form than to the representation of any other class of objects. Obviously so, perhaps, for humans are, after all, animals as opposed to vegetables or minerals. However, while inborn artistic ability, a good eye, technical proficiency, and a knowledge of human anatomy can separately or in various combinations—given the initial ability—result in competence in reproducing the human form in all manner of artistically satisfying ways, no amount of all of these expertises is of much, if any, use in drawing animals unless something else is also available to the artist or depictor. This, moreover, is not just an intimate knowledge of animals or even of their anatomy. It is a very particular kind of familiarity with and attitude toward them, one that is probably almost wholly subjective and in some ways, perhaps, subliminal.

Hardly any two humans are alike, and the human form varies in a most bewildering manner, yet a human being is a human being in general build, despite a few portrait photographs of some great apes that I have seen, which even zoologists at first assumed were people made up as apes. Nobody mistakes a depiction of a man, however crude, distorted, or formalized, for anything else. And herein lies the core of our whole problem. Human beings are not defined only by a set of taxonomic factors, such as being bipedal, having five fingers and toes, and long, straight hind limbs and short fore ones. Lots of other animals display one or more of these characteristics, and some come very close to having all of our rather special anatomical features. Yet human beings do have something that is special; something that is universal to their species, be the individual a steatopygous Bushman, a pot-bellied Mongol, or a Caucasoid string bean. So does every other individual species of animal.

If a depictor—and he need not be an artist in any way —of the human form appreciates this "something" and can get it on a rock face, on paper, or on any other surface, or can model it in clay or chip it out of a block of stone, he or she will be able to communicate to others "man the animal." This, however, does not mean that he will be able to transmit such a "message" of any other animal. What then is this "something"? Can it be defined and how may one go about looking for it? I think it can be defined, and I feel the best way to do this is to recount

how I stumbled across it myself, for I didn't go out looking for it, I have never met anybody who did, and I
certainly didn't suspect its existence before I did come
across it.

I have been assured that at an early age I gave rise to
the usual quota of green cows on purple fields (tangen-
tially, it is rather interesting to note that the extremely
youthful seem instinctively to know that the shadows in
green grass are purple). Since I was brought up much on
the sea, I also gave birth to many smoking ships perched
on aqueous horizons, and this brought my artistic career
to its first stop, for I could not see why said ships should
be moved halfway down the page into the foreground.
After all, they were not supposed to be sinking and, since
I could not see the logic of adulthood in this matter of
perspective, I rather aggressively abandoned colored
pencils for a slingshot, a bent pin, and a butterfly net.

It seems, however, that I was born with a particular
interest in animals, and when I got to Eton I became
entangled in the business of depicting them once more.
It happened thuswise. Eton had a perfectly fiendish prac-
tice of assigning a "summer task." This was a work load
arbitrarily imposed and dictatorially enforced, to be un-
dertaken during the long summer vacation, but which
took up almost as much time as the holidaying itself. You
lost marks and got beaten if you did not perform the
allotted chore. However, everybody was offered a choice
of subjects and one of these was called "art." In this
category one had to produce a quota of original pictures
of specified size and complexity, on a variety of subjects.
The three categories assigned in my first year were boats,
people, and animals—my three pet subjects.

It took me all summer, and I found it rather fun. I was in and out of Plymouth harbor on a yacht that summer, and the famous old clipper ship the *Cutty Sark* was then anchored there and still fully rigged. I copied her with geometric precision, from a rowboat [see Figure 24]. But we also went to Scotland, and I was taken out deer stalking. By some extraordinary fluke I plugged a magnificent stag, though I couldn't hit a barn at a hundred paces, and the creature was so beautiful that I gave up hunting then and there and decided to try to draw its head [see Figure 25]. On the way home from Scotland, I was taken to a race meeting and became greatly intrigued with the bookies. I picked a raucous fat fellow in a derby hat and a violently checked suit, and "did him up brown" that night on a large sheet of rather flabby paper as my last stint.

On judgment day I received the second setback to the flowering of any artistic ability I might have been born with. The judges at first praised all my efforts and, in fact, singled them out in each class; but, when it came time to put the little gold tags on the winners, they announced that they were not awarding mine any prizes because they "had obviously been done from photographs." Apart from anything else, I had never heard anything to the effect that one was not allowed to copy from photographs and, in any case, for one of mine I had not even had a model before me—the bookie. I aggressively abandoned any form of art for some time.

Once on the *City of Baroda* I found time hanging rather heavy on occasion and, being much taken by my little Indian doctor, decided to try my hand at drawing his portrait. When I had finished it I showed it to him—and very nearly gave up art permanently: his first question was, Where did you get the photograph to work from? This crisis was, however, successfully resolved, and the good doctor encouraged me to continue with my drawing.

As I have explained, I had made the objective of my enforced travels the collection of rats and some other small animals, including insects, for the British Museum. I had accumulated quite a lot during my wanderings in Ceylon and upper Malaya, and I had come thereby face-to-face with a singular problem. I knew the animals I had collected only from pictures in books—if I knew them at all—and they did not look in life at all like their published portraits. I have always leaned to a view of animals that is realistic and alive, rather than stuffed and pickled, and I was well nigh horrified at the wild discrepancy between their appearance, habits, and behavior in life from that of their preserved remains in museums and in the written material about their believed or presumed conduct. Since anything mechanical is a complete puzzle to me and a camera an absolute enigma,* I had no means of recording visually most of what I wanted to record of these animals except by trying to draw them. This I had started to do by holding the dead animal in my left hand and sketching what I call its "spare parts" in a school notebook. Later, I had made attempts to depict the whole animals as I had seen them while still alive, from

---

*This latter inability was due in large part to Ivan's very poor eyesight; he could not see through a view finder with either his reading or his long-distance eyeglasses. This did not, however, prevent him from giving advice to photographers, usually to the extent of driving them straight up the wall. [S. W. S.]

memory. The results had not satisfied me at all. It was Achi who taught me the "something" essential to the proper and satisfactory depiction of animals.

There was no art-supply store in Singapore or even in Batavia, as the very civilized capital of Java was then called, and I had not really envisaged drawing anything when I left England, so my only recourse was to go to the local school systems for the necessary materials. The tropics being what they then were, this resulted in the acquisition of nothing more than soft pencils that got hard in the dampness of the jungle, erasers that got slimy and smeared things, and low-grade paper that either got wet and flabby or dry and wrinkled in the most amazing manner once it was unwrapped. Thus my expertise was almost as closely circumscribed as that of a school child of the late Roman Empire armed only with palette and stylus. Ink was impossible, and paints, even if obtainable along with all the paraphernalia they entail, never entered my mind because I couldn't "paint." Besides, you cannot *paint* anything worthwhile of the underside of a mouse's foot unless you can paint miniatures or can blow the things up several times. I could do neither.

So, again, I just held my dead rat on its back with my left hand, and the pencil in my right, and endeavored to place a depiction, natural size, of the underside of the foot (let us say) of the rat on a piece of (usually) gently wavy, low-quality paper, of a somewhat soggy consistency. Drawing boards there were not, because any made of wood soft enough to get a thumbtack into warped in the wet forest air. Thus the paper had to be flat on a table. As the table was invariably warped too, one achieved some rather remarkable effects; fortunately Nature is not much for straight lines. I just scratched away, trying not to push the mysteriously hardened soft pencil point through the equally mysteriously softened hard paper. It was a most tiresome and tedious process, because very often the so-called table was a rickety structure made of the midribs of palm fronds, while the rats died in the traps only at night, and illumination was seldom more than a bush lamp, the glass of which smoked up in the slightest draft. One could hardly call this art school, but one learned—indeed one did!

So much for the most essential work—viz., the "spare parts" of the animals needed for the scientific record. The less essential aspect of my drawing activities was less tedious and, in fact, rather relaxing. This was the whole animal. And it was with these that I learned my first real lesson in drawing animals.

I have never drawn whole animals from models. I don't see how it could be done, because animals are seldom seen in the wild and then only for fleeting moments, and the wretched things are always moving. Therefore, I had developed the habit of obtaining as many animals as possible and keeping them alive for a time in cages or tethered, in order to observe them. Then, in time off from the "spare parts" department, I would take a larger piece of paper and try to record my impressions of the beasts as I had done with my doctor friend. But to my surprise and considerable chagrin I discovered that I could not capture the precise species I wanted to depict. What I mean is, all cats in the generic sense came out like domestic cats [see Figure 23], buffalo like old cows, elephants like Medieval paintings of those creatures, and most birds like nothing more than variously ornamented blackbirds. What was even worse, creatures such as Civets also came out basically "cats," simply with longer tails and funnier faces. Then something struck me. The faces!

Now, faces constitute a "spare part," and it dawned on me quite abruptly one day that *all* my drawings of animals since the green-cow-on-purple-field days had been of "spare parts"—never anything more than a portrait. The bodies of all the animals that I now tried to portray, invariably had a standard body line. Though I had spent all my life looking at animals, I had apparently always taken this for granted. To push the simile, a steamship is a steamship apart from the number of funnels it has, and a car is a car, though a Rolls-Royce has a different "face" from a Bentley, a Ford, or a Bugatti. Further, with animals I was, for the first time, being confronted with items not included in the standard European lines, not even in zoos.

This failing I immediately tried to rectify, but the results were only a very slight improvement. Civets still looked like cats. This puzzled me until Achi, who was my severest critic, asked me why I always started by drawing the body. I had never realized this. I pondered the remark, and it slowly dawned upon me that I had been treating the body itself as a spare part, building it first, just as I would a car, and ending off with the grill. Then I tried a new tack and stumbled upon what I consider to be a most important factor in drawing animals. This is, draw the head first and finish it up to the point where the expression is absolutely right, then work backward, in whichever direction seems best, building the body. Leave the spare parts to the end; draw them separately;

and then tack them on, using tracing paper transfers if necessary.

This procedure brought about a most encouraging improvement, and at first I congratulated myself on having achieved success to my complete satisfaction. However, Achi was still far from satisfied. He found it hard to express himself, and not only because of the language difficulty—neither basic English nor kitchen Malay is devised to express the higher flights of artistic nuance. He did get over to me, however, the simple fact that my whole-animal drawings were wrong—specifically, that is. "Those two kinds of squirrels," Achi eventually spelled out, "look the same on paper except for their faces, yet they look quite different." Once this fact was pointed out to me, I perceived it to be only too true. What on earth was wrong? And again it was Achi who led me to the next and most important of all factors in drawing animals. What he did was this:

"Look," he said, speaking of one member of the civet tribe called a Musang. "He sit like this, not like that"; and he wove his hands and arms into a combined graceful curve. It struck me like a thunderbolt. By Jove, the creature *did* sit just like that. I could actually visualize its body filling out around Achi's arms.

"How else does it sit?" I remember demanding in great excitement.

"Oh, like this, or this, or . . ."

"Stop!" I actually shouted. "Do that again."

When he did so, holding the last pose, I walked around him looking at that graceful curve from all angles. No doubt about it, that was still a *Musang*.

"Now make the *Burong Aüt*," I told him. This was his

name for the Hemigale, another member of the civet tribe that I had tried to draw.

Achi waved his arms about quite a bit, fluttered his fingers like a Balinese dancer, thought some, and then adopted another stance. And, *Py Jinkoa*, I'd have sworn that I was looking at a Hemigale sitting composedly on a branch. So I went to work under the gimlet eye of my first and only art teacher and thus came upon what I still believe to be one of the greatest discoveries of the age. I call it simply "The Line."

This I would never have discovered for myself, and I have often wondered if it was inborn in little Achi. His people, like all Malays, are incredibly "artistic," to use the word in its widest and nicer sense, and he certainly knew his animals. He was even able to demonstrate the "lines" of animals he had never seen before after only a few moments observation of them *alive*. Here was a seeming paradox plus a strange enigma; and it was these that led me to my next discovery. This is simply that you'll never draw animals unless you happen to have been born what we call an "animal person."

This has nothing to do with "loving" animals—a phrase which is, in my opinion, an abomination—and it need not have much to do with "knowing" about them; a lot of zoologists are very far from being animal persons. Rather it is, I think, something to do with what has come to be called in general (and misleadingly) psychology. Very few people *dislike* animals per se, though almost all of us have a *bête-noire*, such as snakes. Mine happens to be spiders, but even this does not dampen my *interest* in these, though I must admit to being able to give myself the cold shivers when I am drawing one. Then, at least, I know that I am getting the creature "right."

This "line" is not just the backbone, because it applies also to animals without backbones. It is not the *outline* of the animal either. It is internal and apparently invisible to all but animal persons, though the great majority of other people seem to be able to spot its absence or its misapplication quite readily. All I can tell you is that from that day on it has been my starting point for all my animal drawings. The procedure I devised goes as follows:

First I look at the animal alive for as long as I can spare the time. Then I go away from it and fiddle around till I get its particular line on paper. This is usually in profile. Next, I draw the face from whatever angle I want, starting with the eyes—at the appropriate end of the line, of course. Around the eyes I build the head, working outward. If I don't get the expression right the first time, I toss the thing out and start again. I then build the rest of the body around this "chassis." And the line *is*, in a manner, a chassis.

This phase ends with a semicompleted outline, lacking hands and feet, horns, and other such spare parts. These I draw separately in great detail, often from field work done on a dead specimen or from scale photographs. There are sub-lines in these, which you have to get used to in changing their position vis-à-vis the angle of vision. These done, I trace them off and twiddle them around the appropriate point on the body until I get their pitch and yaw right, if I may use these terms. Having thus completed my outline, I sit down to the really ticklish part, though not without pleasurable expectations.

This is coloring the thing in, or "doing it up brown," or whatever you want to call it; and the ticklish part is that you may wreck the whole thing at almost any stage before completion for, you see, there is the expression to be developed, and this is in both the face *and* the body. How often have I got a perfect outline drawing and then completely muffed this? One wrong stroke in or around an eye will do it, and I have found it practically impossible to correct it by erasure. Something goes permanently wrong.

Then there is the texture of the surface to be considered. Mammals' fur varies enormously in texture; birds' feathers are pure hell; reptiles' scales are murder, since they change size and shape by abstruse mathematical progressions that can play havoc with perspective; fish are even worse in this respect—there are all manner of different degrees of shininess, and there is iridescence and even luminescence. Color also has many different sets of qualities that, when depicting animals, are of the essence and especially when you are working in black and white. Muff any of these and you won't get a true picture, and I insist that drawings of animals should be as nearly true (like a photograph) as possible, and at this stage you may well miss or botch the overall *expression.* And I cannot overemphasize the importance of expression.

How do I get these "expressions" into my drawings? Please, I do not wish to sound bombastic, but how was the expression of the *Mona Lisa* achieved? You may answer "genius" to that one, but don't apply it to me. The ability is definitely inborn, not learned, so there's nothing clever about it. I'm sure Leonardo da Vinci could do it deliberately, and that *is* genius; I have to fiddle around for hours until it comes naturally, and if it doesn't, I'm stymied. The only advantage I do have is that I was born an "animal person," so I know when I *have* got it right.

Depicting animals requires first not only a knowledge of animals, their characters and characteristics, and their habits, but also some kind of inborn sympathy for or empathy with them. Secondly, you must *draw* your animal first and get its basic individual line right and then get all its spare parts right, also in line. Only then attempt to "do it up brown," which means actually "painting" in its texture, substance, and perspective by shading, coloring, and the designing of a background, foreground, and shadows. The pose is an outcome of the line, and thus of the drawing; the expression, for the most part, comes out of this secondary process. However, there are those, mostly Orientals, who can get the latter into the former. This is the ideal I strive for, and I will repeat something I said earlier: this is that the expression is as much in the whole body as in the face and in its paramount feature—the eyes.

The drawings included here, even those of animals I saw only in the East Indies, were done many years after my trip there, but they are still the result of Achi's tutelage. I shall always carry in my mind's eye the picture of Achi sitting Hemigale-wise.

❧ 13 ❧

Ternate, Halmahera, and the Aru Islands:
The Birds of Paradise

I DON'T KNOW WHY CERTAIN
names have the effect they do. For me, Macassar spelt
tropics, and I had always yearned to visit the place. Halmahera was another. Had it still been known as Gilolo,
as Wallace called it (the Portuguese name), I know I
would not have gone to nearly so much trouble as I did
to get there. Gilolo meant nothing to me, but Halmahera
was redolent of sandalwood and spices, tropical breezes,
and exotic fauna.

Politically, Halmahera is part of Ternate, which small
island lying off its west coast is much more important
[see Figure 26]. Indeed, even today, knowledge of Halmahera is very incomplete. It is mountainous with at
least one active volcano, Gam Kenora, and must have
had an interesting geological history. There are coral

formations on the heights, numerous rivers (though none of great importance), and a number of respectably sized lakes. Too, near Weda, just south of the great eastern-pointing arm of Halmahera, there is the Grotto of Sagea, a stalactite grotto that rivals the famous Blue Grotto of Capri.

There is prolific vegetation but, as I knew from Wallace's book, the coast opposite Ternate is largely a plain covered with tall, coarse grass, the forests being considerably inland. Through the kindness of a Dutch resident I did manage a short trip to Dodinga, a village on a bay opposite Ternate, where Wallace spent some time. None of the local people I talked to had any but the vaguest handed-down recollections of Wallace, but they took me to the path he had described as crossing this very narrow isthmus—here only two miles in width—and Achi and I trod, literally, as we told ourselves, in the footsteps of my idol. Such is the romanticism of youth!

This path was a very good one and was much used to bring produce from villages on the east coast to those on the west coast and vice versa, but the surrounding forest was luxuriant, and I wished for time to explore it properly. We dared not leave the path without a guide, for the terrain was very rugged, great limestone boulders jutting out everywhere and providing rather precarious footing. I did not relish the idea of a broken ankle or worse, and we had not brought proper collecting gear with us in any case. We did catch some insects, which were carried back to the village in a distinctly odd assortment of containers concocted from anything we had on us that could be made to serve that purpose. There were birds in plenty, but I did not ever collect these and could not even put a name to those we saw except to identify them as parrots or lories or as "thrushlike" or some other unhelpful designation.

I actually had two reasons for traveling to Ternate and Halmahera, the first simply to be able to say I had been there if only for a brief time, but second, and far more important, to get to the Aru Islands [see Figure 27]. Here I was frankly very lucky. No one had been able to tell me what means I might find to cross the sea to the Aru Islands, since there was no regular boat service, and I did not have the money to hire a boat and crew even at the low rates that prevailed. By inquiring around I narrowed down the possibilities until they appeared to be completely nonexistent; and even the normally in-genious Achi had no luck, which made me gloomier than ever. But the Fates were kind, or perhaps not looking in my direction.

Ternate is quite "civilized" and really very pleasant indeed, with lovely views on every side, and I took to walking on the rather extensive beach instead of glower-ing about the town. At the end of one lap I became aware of a person of obvious Chinese descent and absolutely monumental proportions apparently waiting for some-thing near one of the docks. As I drew closer he beck-oned to me, and from sheer politeness I went over to him. Without any preamble at all, he announced, "We are going to the Aru Islands." It was some moments before I realized that the "we" was neither royal nor editorial but meant "us," "you and me," and included Achi and Nona as well. There was one small catch here; I had about a half hour to settle my account at the hotel, pack my bags and get them to the dock, etc., etc., and

Achi knew nothing of our sudden good fortune. I wasn't even certain that he was at the hotel; but my luck held.

Whether my Chinese benefactor, Mr. Wong by name, had sent messages, or whether the manager was just superbly efficient I am not certain, but Achi got my baggage all packed and onto a cart with nearly the speed of light, and I had all the business details—including an ecstatic cable to my mother—concluded in time to scramble on board. Having joyfully watched the shoreline retreating and having caught my breath somewhat, I had time to look around me. To my dismay, this prau, for it was basically a prau, looked hardly seaworthy. It was much smaller than the one in which I sailed from Bali and appeared to be in rather bad repair, but its looks proved deceiving, and we made the trip without difficulty. Of course, we hit no storms either.

The crew was composed of Ternate Malays with a Chinese captain; and the owner's wife, as tiny as her husband was enormous, was also on board. She spoke excellent English, and I judged her to be very upper class and wondered how she came to be a merchant's wife on a rather remote island—he had told me that he was the third generation to carry on the family business there. I could not, of course, ask her for an explanation, but I never got over the feeling that she belonged under glass. Even in her relatively "rough" clothing she was exquisite. She was also exceedingly shrewd. As we neared the shore, she asked me rather casually how long I intended to stay. I was a bit perplexed and said I really didn't know; whereupon she dealt me the softest hammer blow I've ever experienced: she asked quietly, "How will you get back then?"

It will, of course, have been perfectly obvious to anyone reading this book that a one-way trip to such an out-of-the-way place was not what I should have been looking for, but in fact I had been so intent on just getting *to* the Aru Islands that I never gave any thought to getting *back*. Mr. Wong would spend two or three days there trading and would then return to Ternate. This I knew was not nearly enough time. I looked around at Achi, who went absolutely inscrutable on me and proceeded to examine the sky. Mr. Wong also looked inscrutable and completely unhelpful. Silently calling on all my ancestors, direct and collateral, for help, I said as confidently as I could that I would certainly manage somehow. (After all, I was British and had been to Eton, and the honor of the Empire was at stake!) They all, including Achi, nodded solemnly—and then burst out laughing. When they had recovered from their mirth, Mr. Wong hastened to reassure me. Some of what he said was, in retrospect, not very flattering but his phrasing was so ingenious that I didn't realize it at the time.

The gist of it was that everyone else had realized that there was a slight flaw in my plans. Indeed, it had been Achi who had gone privately to Mr. Wong and asked discreetly about transport *from* the Aru Islands, being somewhat concerned that he might never see his homeland again if I were left in charge. But surely I must know that it is much easier to get to the Aru Islands from Macassar via Ceram, since traders sail to and fro with considerable regularity. Certainly I might have to wait a bit, but I would not be permanently stranded, and living on these islands would cost me very little.

Mr. Wong also, with really great magnanimity and no

fuss, refused to accept any payment for either our passage or the meals he had supplied us.

You are undoubtedly wondering by now just why I was so very intent on visiting these islands that, probably, you have never heard of. As I have mentioned, the great Alfred Russel Wallace was my childhood idol, and I hoped to follow in his footsteps, both figuratively and, on this trip, as literally as possible. He wrote of his stay there as follows:

> My expedition to the Aru Islands had been eminently successful. . . . I had made the acquaintance of a strange and little-known race of men; I had become familiar with the traders of the far East; I had revelled in the delights of exploring a new fauna and flora, one of the most remarkable and most beautiful and least-known in the world; and I had succeeded in the main object for which I had undertaken the journey—namely, to obtain fine specimens of the magnificent Birds of Paradise, and to be enabled to observe them in their native forests. By this success I was stimulated to continue my researches in the Moluccas and New Guinea for nearly five years longer, and it is still the portion of my travels to which I look back with the most complete satisfaction.*

I have deliberately left out part of this quotation and will return to it later.

I did not collect birds, but I was eager to see the Birds of Paradise in their natural haunts and to visit another of Wallace's dwelling places. Here we were again in luck. Several of the natives knew of him from their parents or grandparents, and one very elderly gentleman claimed he actually remembered Wallace! He must have been a very small boy when Wallace

---

* *The Malay Archipelago* (London 1869; Dover reprint 1962), p. 369.

was there,* but his comments led me to credit his statement. In any case, Wallace's book, *The Malay Archipelago*,
described his route in detail, naming even the smallest
villages in which he stayed. What I was looking for was
not a village per se but a "place" on a creek on one of
the islands, and these people were able not just to direct
me but actually to lead me there.

To go back a bit, I should tell you something of these
magic islands. They lie just south of New Guinea—technically, West Irian—and are unique in many ways. On a
map they look like a large island that has been hacked
into several pieces, "rivers" separating the fragments.
These "rivers" are actually salt-water channels ten to
fifteen fathoms [60 to 80 feet] deep, with no current, and
are bordered on each side by banks and cliffs, with forest
above. They are called rivers on some maps, though they
are not, despite even their appearance at close hand. A
few small streams do feed into them. The islands are
generally low—probably not over 200 feet anywhere—
but undulating and rocky. The rocks are coralline, and
there is much coral in the adjacent shallow seas. The
"rivers" are their most unusual feature, and Wallace
speculated that the Aru Islands were once part of New
Guinea (only 150 miles away) and that the "rivers" were
indeed once rivers, but that the whole was included in a
general subsidence in that area, the Aru Islands remaining on the "outskirts" of this and sinking only slightly,
so retaining nearly their usual level. No other explana-

---

*Wallace visited the Aru Islands in 1856 and 1857, and Ivan was
there in 1928. Presumably, therefore, the old gentleman was
about eighty, a most respectable age for someone in that area but
by no means impossible. [S. W. S.]

tion seems to account for the regular depth and width or the winding course of these channels. Too, the fauna of the Aru Islands and of New Guinea are closely linked, including such as the wingless Cassowary and other purely terrestrial birds, and some species are unique to these islands. Other islands no further from New Guinea than are the Aru Islands do not share their fauna.

Our guides and bearers took us along the River Wateiai, which divides the main island, Maykor, from its northern neighbor, Wokan. We then turned south along a creek, finally halting at a clearing containing a house of sorts, which they insisted was that occupied by Wallace. This is most improbable, since the original was apparently in none too good shape and would have rotted several times between Wallace's visit and mine, but I do believe that this was the place where Wallace stayed.

What I wanted most to see was the gathering of the Great Bird of Paradise (*Paradisaea apoda**) that Wallace had described. The author was a bit vague about the exact date when this display took place, but by studying his itinerary and questioning the natives we felt sure that we had arrived at the right time.

There was a very large and tall tree not far from the clearing in which our house stood, and I decided that this was the very tree mentioned by Wallace. We heard Birds of Paradise—their cries are not beautiful, and they are

---

Apoda means "footless" and resulted from the fact that the first skins received by scientists in Europe came initially from native collectors whose habit it was to chop off the feet, only the skins being wanted by the traders, who bought them for purely commercial reasons.

actually close relatives of the Crow, a fact more indicated by their voices than their plumage—but saw nothing of them until we went further into the forest, when we did catch glimpses of them far above us. This tree not having yielded results, we set out each morning just before dawn, entering the forest in a different direction each time but in no case going very far.

Finally, we were rewarded. Literally dozens of these gorgeous birds assembled above us and, fluffing out their plumes of golden orange, bobbed and bowed and strutted about on the bare branches, while the dull-colored females pecked around below, apparently indifferent to the display above. The male Great Birds of Paradise in full plumage are magnificent. This is the largest species known, being some seventeen inches long from the beak to the tip of the tail. The body, wings, and tail are a rich coffee brown, while the top of the head and the neck is a delicate yellow. The lower part of the throat up to the eye is an almost iridescent metallic emerald green, with even deeper green in a band across the forehead and the chin. The beak is a pale lead blue, the eyes yellow, and the feet a pale pink. The two major tail feathers may be from two to almost three feet in length and are wirelike. And from under each wing there springs a dense tuft of long and delicate plumes, an incredible golden orange in color, changing into a pale brown toward the tips. These plumes can be spread out at will and nearly hide the bird.

Imagine, then, a host of these birds, vibrating their plumes and darting from branch to branch, now and again bowing their bodies, the yellow head and green throat set off against the fairy plumes above. Achi and I did not speak but only watched until the birds departed and then walked silently back.

In those days, Birds of Paradise were exported in great numbers for the milliners of Paris, London, and New York, but already someone had taken an interest in their preservation and instituted the world's strangest colony. This, probably the most extraordinary example of planned settlement the world has ever seen, is on a tiny island with an area of only 250 acres, situated in the blue Caribbean. This colony is highly successful and has a most romantic history fraught with undertones of mystery, horror, and gentle beauty. All the colonists are Great Birds of Paradise.*

This story began in the year 1909 when a very remarkable man named Sir William Ingram, wealthy owner of British newspapers and large cacao estates in the West Indian island of Trinidad, became worried about the plight of these wonderful birds, which were being slaughtered at the most horrible rate. In one year as many as 30,000 were traded on a London market alone, while in another year a single shipment of over 28,000 reached that port. Sir William not only deplored this trade in all its aspects but he also decided to do something about it.

He therefore acquired the services of two Englishmen and sent them to the Aru Islands. These are specifically the home of the Great Bird of Paradise, although they are also found on New Guinea. The two collectors were

---

*In all, there are forty-three species of Birds of Paradise.

instructed to catch as many of these as possible and to take them to England.

Their collecting was very successful, and nearly sixty birds were captured. This was accomplished with the help of the local natives, who for years had been capturing the birds by a unique method. Since the skins were of great value but their feathers were very delicate, shooting the birds with either gun or arrow ruined their plumage. The Aru Islanders had therefore developed a method of shooting them with long arrows bearing little conical wooden cups attached in place of arrowheads, and with the open end pointing forward. These only stunned the birds and knocked them to the ground. When collecting for commercial purposes, the natives constructed little platforms in special trees where the male birds congregated to perform their displays or dances.

When the birds had been captured, one of the collectors set out for England, where Sir William was waiting hopefully but not too sanguinely to receive his precious brood. This poor collector, however, had a real problem on his hands, for the birds were not only used to tropical conditions but also demanded a somewhat specialized and troublesome diet. They were omnivorous, like ourselves, but required live insects and fresh fruit. Luckily, however, there happened to be among the ship's crew a strange man by the name of Robert Herold, who said that he was Swiss and who immediately took matters in hand. By an assiduous and continuous search for cockroaches and by safaris ashore at each port of call in quest of grapes, this odd man made it possible for the collector to land triumphantly in England with all his charges alive and in good health.

However, Sir William's troubles were not over. Problems still faced him, one of which was the continuing necessity for fresh grapes and live cockroaches. It was midwinter, and in England in this season both items are scarce, while a constant flow of live cockroaches to satisfy the needs of sixty large, hungry birds is not, at the best of times, a slender order. However, the whole family and a host of minions cooperated, and the birds were somehow fed and managed to thrive until they reached their new home in the sunny West Indies.

This was the tiny island paradise off the northeastern coast of Tobago, and known as Little Tobago. Tobago itself is a dependency of Trinidad, which lies off the north coast of South America, where the great arc of the West Indies meets that continent. Little Tobago is like a Pacific island in miniature. The north shore is steep and piled with broken chunks of coral, bathed in salty spray, and fringed by a grove of cactuses. The body of the island consists of four conical peaks—the highest just short of 500 feet—and it is clothed in thick, lush tropical growth. In the gulleys and ravines the trees reach a tremendous height in search of air and light. The vegetation is full of beautiful Fan Palms and enormous, cabbagelike things known locally and appropriately as "big-leaves," which grow on the ground, on rocks, and even on the trees. Their leaves are often over seven feet long. The profusion of plant things is inconceivable to those who have not seen the great equatorial forests. Here and there, tremendous Cabbage Palms send their great green cylinders towering aloft on smooth, pillarlike gray trunks, and the wild plums, fiddlewood, and pimentos are loaded with vines and parasitic plants to their very leaftips.

Little Tobago lies two and a half miles from its big brother, Tobago, and in the channel between, which is whipped into a race by contrary prevailing winds and a strong current, lies a group of rocks known as "The Goats." Its climate is almost identical to that of the Aru Islands, and it is on almost exactly the opposite side of the earth. The whole island had been purchased by Sir William as a paradise for his paradisaical colonists.

Little Tobago was uninhabited—that is to say, by men. However, here comes the first undertone of that mystery that seems to haunt this story—a drollery so typical of the Spanish Main in its best tradition—for the island was inhabited by a myriad of "ghost" chickens. In the morning, innumerable cocks made the forest ring with their crowing, and as the chance visitor crept about the undergrowth, he could hear hens clucking and chicks peeping on all sides. The slightest disturbance, however, caused these familiar noises to cease. The perpetrators were not seen. Nevertheless, for all their ghostly behavior, they were real enough. They were fowls, all right, but not the gawking, clucking, silly, barnyard creatures we know, for they had reverted not only in habits, but actually in plumage, to a close semblance of their far off ancestors in the jungles of India. They were descendants of fowls put upon the island in 1870 by the irate inhabitants of a village on nearby Tobago, along with some goats, a dog, and an inebriate! The story is a bit bizarre.

Apparently a man named Mitchell had become such a hopeless drunk that his friends dumped him, with this small menagerie, on Little Tobago—which one cannot get off without a boat, because of the strong currents. They called once a week to bring the man some meagre supplies. Then, after some years, there came a day when the visiting party was met on the little sandy landing cove only by the dog which, with a wild barking, immediately dashed off into the bush. The visitors followed, and the little dog led them right across the island to the windward side, where the Atlantic surf beats ceaselessly upon the coral rocks. There he showed them an old tattered coat with some fishing line and three large fish completely dried out by the strong sun and curved over a rock. For the rest, there was only the pounding of the waves, the steady sunlight, and the sighing of the trade winds in the sea-grape bushes. Mitchell had gone, his exact fate never determined. The little dog went back to the main island with the visitors, the goats lingered on for some years and then died out, but the fowls went to bush and multiplied exceedingly.

When Sir William's colonists were released in September of 1909, there were other natural inhabitants of the island; birds of many kinds, lizards, innumerable insects, and a multitude of snails and lesser beasts were found everywhere. However, there were no rats, opossums, or other mammals, and no snakes, so that, apart from hawks that sailed over from the mainland, there were no wild inhabitants that might be harmful to the immigrants from the East Indies. The colonists were established at a little camp on the lee side of the island, along with the strange Swiss sailor Robert Herold, who had refused to abandon his charges in London and who now insisted upon being left alone to care for them.

At first the birds were kept in cages and fed with bananas and pawpaws—a tropical, vegetable-marrow-shaped fruit that grows on little single-stemmed trees with a crown of spreading leaves and of which there was a small, overgrown field on the island. Then they were let out to search for insects, but they apparently did not do so well, and Herold says in his first report to Sir William Ingram that he caught them all again—though how he does not say!—and transported them and his temporary abode to another glade at the other end of the island. Here they were again let out and immediately took happily to the trees, feeding on the wild cherries and plums and finding an abundance of insects to suit their tastes. They took to the same food as the local Orioles, their distant relatives, and were even observed robbing small birds' nests of their eggs and young. Everything seemed to be going according to plan, but there were still two worries haunting Sir William, who was solely responsible for the whole project and who bore all its expenses from the inception in 1909 until the day of his death fifteen years later.

First, although the climate of the island is damp and rain occurs plentifully during nine months of the year, there are three months of dry weather when there is no water on the island apart from small rain pools. However, during the wet season the birds found their own water in hollows in trees, and Herold discovered one pool on top of a rock that contained enough good water to serve him and the birds during the dry season. He drew this off to a tank by cutting away the rock.

Sir William's other cause for concern was much more disturbing. Unfortunately, the Great Birds of Paradise, for all the flamboyant beauty of the mature males, are just button-eyed, inquisitive, and rather rowdy brown birds for the first five or six years of their lives. Moreover, during this time the hens look just like the cocks. The whole of Mr. Herold's brood were young birds, and Sir William has described in unmistakable terms his gloomy ponderings upon their eventual proclivities. Were there any females among the lot? There was no way of telling and, what is more, females are scarce in nature, and the natives had become accustomed to hunting the males, which lead somewhat different lives and have slightly different habits.

After a few deaths at the very beginning—two resulting from a fight and at least three others from unknown causes—the colonists seem to have settled down happily, but hardly quietly, for they are noisy, quarrelsome birds. Robert Herold tended them devotedly, clearing paths across the island so that he could patrol their domain, warn off the strangers who never came, and carry water daily to the different communities that had established themselves about the island.

In July 1913 Herold reported seeing three young birds with their mother, and Sir William's greatest worry was resolved. Either among the original forty-eight birds that finally reached Little Tobago, or three that had subsequently been released, there had been females. Many males were by this time in their full, glorious plumage. They got out of gear for a time, breeding and moulting at the wrong season, but as time went on they recovered their normal seasonal periodicity, and by 1918 they were quite back to normal.

After seven years, Robert Herold died. This sounds a

natural enough thing for any man to do, but again the underlying romance of this little colony manifested itself. Herold, on his death bed, confessed that he was neither a seaman nor a Swiss and announced that he was the son of a famous Bohemian professor. He explained that he had run away to avoid service under the hated Austrians in whose power his country had lain helpless for so long, and to avoid the war that he saw to be inevitable. He had preferred to devote his life to the care of some beautiful, angry birds on a tiny, tropical island. Had he lived another four years, he would have seen his country liberated.

With the passing of Herold, the history of the colony moved swiftly and dramatically, though the birds were doubtless never aware of the fact. A new caretaker was appointed. He was a local man, and he averted loneliness by taking with him to Little Tobago his son and, most unwisely, somebody else's wife. The subsequent events ran true to Caribbean form.

An irate husband promptly invaded the island paradise, killed the renegade wife, hunted down the man's son and slew him in the recesses of the jungle paths, and then stalked the wretched sinner himself. When he finally cornered him, he beat him to what he thought was death, and then calmly left the island. With customary and maddening imperturbability the records entirely neglect to mention how or why the hapless fellow was found, but he was rescued and removed. Another man was appointed in his place.

This man was an ex-policeman and seems to have been quite the antithesis of his predecessor. He was a man of considerable intelligence and acute powers of observation. His reports to Sir William were regular and even more detailed than Herold's, and he seems to have taken his job very seriously. He watered the birds daily and kept down the hawks. He noted many young birds and saw hens carrying straw and twigs in their beaks, but although he searched continually, he never found a nest. This seems to have annoyed, even exasperated, him, as he constantly refers to it in his reports. He also says several times toward the end that the birds were increasing so rapidly that he fully expected the island to be composed of solid Birds of Paradise before long if they did not reach the main island.

Sir William left Little Tobago to his widow when he died in 1924, but she died in 1928, and a deed was then drawn up conveying the island and all its bird colonists to the Government of Trinidad. It has since been visited by many famous naturalists, who have reported that the birds were very much in evidence, healthy, active, and apparently continuing to increase in numbers. They can be heard from the sea as one approaches the island, "whaaking" happily. A system of large water butts was placed in the trees, and a caretaker was dispensed with. Later, fields of fruit trees were planted and a permanent water system was devised by the Government.

Britain may have lost her empire, but she has at least one permanently contented colony to her credit.

And I have never forgotten that morning on Maykor in the Aru Islands. The rising sun burnished the sky behind the green filigree of the foliage, its hard rays lancing through the dark greenery, glinting on the smooth-trunked trees, and bathing the eastern faces of their silvery limbs like light from the open mouth of a furnace. The sky above was blue, shot with a luminous tomato-colored overtone. The air was still and very moist. Everywhere around rose a porous wall of motionlessly writhing vegetation. The ropes of great creepers wove in and out among cascades of fluffy leaves; sprays of palm fronds shot upward; rafts of green, plate-shaped discs jutted forth on every hand; and the intervening spaces were stuffed with luscious, fleshy vegetation that had giant fingers and long shiny spikes. The earth below was dark brown. It looked soft and spongy and had tiny things sticking up in it. The earth smelt damp and clean, and the whole world smelt of the earth. And above all there danced the Birds of Paradise.

❧ 14 ❧

The Aru Islands: Cuscuses, Kangaroos, and Cassowaries

WE STAYED AT THIS CAMP for some days, making forays into the surrounding forest to look for insects and mammals. We saw few mammals, and the first specimen came to me rather than my going to him. This was a Cuscus *(Phalanger)* [see Figure 28] that persisted in coming down out of the trees and climbing into bed with me at dawn for three mornings running. I could not at first bring myself to try to "collect" him, but I persisted in tossing him out and finally had to take very drastic action when he added injury to insult by biting me on the shoulder. The wound was a rather nasty one, and Achi looked a bit perturbed when he examined it. He decreed that it should be allowed to bleed for a bit —which it was doing with considerable enthusiasm anyway—to ensure against infection, and promptly vanished into the forest. He seemed to me to be away for a very long time, and I began to wonder if I would bleed to death, though actually it was only a few minutes before he returned with a handful of leaves which he crushed and bound over the wound with part of one of my remaining good shirts. I have no idea what they were, and Achi could tell me only a native name, which proved to be unknown to botanists I talked with later, but the wound healed rapidly and left no visible scar.

The Cuscuses are marsupials, which means that they possess pouches into which they put their babies, usually four in number, when they are very small. Scientists call the Cuscuses *Phalangers,* but that is the English name of another kind of animal, a relative of the Cuscuses, which the Australians call opossums. These latter and the real Opossum, which is an inhabitant of the Americas only, are marsupials also. The Cuscuses are found over a wide area stretching from the Cape York Peninsula of Queensland in Australia, through New Guinea and on to Timor and Celebes, and come in a rather bewildering variety of colors. The males are usually cream, yellow, or dirty white, with large irregular reddish-brown or black blotches all over their backs. The females, on the other hand, are dingy dark brown or gray with white bellies. But just to make matters difficult, this color changes from island to island, so that in some places both males and females are uniformly dark colored, while in others even the females may be partly spotted with light colors.

The most noticeable thing about Cuscuses is their eyes. These are large and red and have vertical, slit-shaped pupils that can be reduced to a tiny size in bright light like those of cats. Also, their tails are prehensile, which is to say they can be used as a fifth hand to curl around branches and hold on with. The tail is part furred and part naked but is covered with a rasplike arrangement of pointed scales. Most queer of all, though, are the hands and feet, which are naked below, so that the animals walk on soft pads, as we do. The first and second fingers—that is, the thumb and the index finger—are both set off at an angle to the others, unlike our hands where only the thumb is opposed. On the hind feet it is the second and third toes that are not ordinary. They are joined together in a common skin and are somewhat opposed to the rest.

The Cuscuses are generally slow-moving animals, but they are also extraordinarily agile and can, when they want to, spring from branch to branch just like squirrels, which is surprising inasmuch as they are the size of a large cat and are very heavy animals. Their expressions are sleepy, but they have vicious tempers and are very quarrelsome among themselves. They are nocturnal and spend the day curled up, lying on their sides. Their diet consists of fruits, small animals, eggs, and big snails which they find in the tops of the trees and pull out of their shells.

Why such a generally retiring animal should have chosen to try to share my bed, I don't know, but I can state from personal experience that they are nearly as difficult to kill as the Kaguan. Their fur is woolly and very thick, and they literally have thick skins. A blast from my shotgun at really quite close range, though admittedly with small shot, did not apparently do much damage to my unwanted guest. He departed at full speed, hurling imprecations in my direction, and we did not see him again.

There are Striped Phalangers (*Dactylopsila*) in the Arus, but I cannot honestly say I saw any. They are nocturnal and arboreal and may have been among the "things" I squinted at during our walks at dawn and dusk, but the foliage was so thick that it was impossible to get a clear look at whatever it was that was causing the commotion above. We also got brief glimpses of a kangaroo [probably a Pademelon—*Setonyx* or *Thylogale?*] that grazed on a grassy plateau not far from the stream bank every evening. He could move considerably faster than we could and was very nervous, the slightest sound from us sending him darting into a tunnel through dense undergrowth where we could not follow. He was small, probably not more than about two and a half feet long, with a relatively short tail, and appeared rather ratlike in general shape. We tried one morning to trace the tunnel from the outside, as it were, since we could not crawl through the tunnel itself, if only because even a small kangaroo can be very dangerous at close quarters, striking out with its tremendous back claws that can disembowel a man. Hence we worked our way through the undergrowth, thick here because of the more open canopy occasioned by the savannahlike areas strung along this particular ridge, from time to time seeing what we at least thought to be evidence of the tunnel constructed by the kangaroo. We came finally to a not very high but nearly sheer wall and decided to bear to our right around it, expecting to get back toward the tunnel once we had passed it, since it seemed not to extend very far but to be simply an outcropping of rock. I took the lead, for Achi was carrying most of our equipment and did not have both hands free for emergencies.

The first few steps were without incident, and I was contemplating a quick and easy transit when everything gave way under me and I slid none too gently down what proved to be a bank bordering a flat swampy area below us. After that things got a bit complicated. I landed, miraculously enough, with only a few minor scratches, though covered with bits of debris, twigs in my hair, and the like, but minus my glasses. These had been neatly hitched off my nose by a wiry branch as I slid by, and flung away when it sprang back to its normal position.

Now, this was not just serious but nearly catastrophic for me, for I had long ago lost my other pair, and though I had a prescription with me, I had no idea how long it might be before I could get them replaced. I was virtually blind in one eye, having been born with the socket badly misshapen, and the sight in my "good" eye was not a great deal better.

Achi had slithered and scrambled down to rescue me and now proceeded to annoy me unwarrantably by chortling gleefully at finding me unharmed. Eventually I managed to get through to him the fact that we must find my glasses. I didn't dare try to look for them myself since I would have stepped on the blasted things long before I saw them, and I really hadn't the foggiest notion which way they had gone. We tried to determine which the offending branch was, but a few experiments indicated that this wouldn't help anyway, so Achi gave me Nona's leash and began casting slowly back and forth, and I prayed that they had not gone into some kind of sinkhole. This went on for some time, and I became very depressed. Nona had trundled around for a bit and then came to sit in my lap with her arms around my neck, hooting gently in my ear with increasing insistance, so that I finally turned to take a look at her, only to let out a shout, sending poor Achi about four feet in the air. He returned at the double, convinced that I had been bitten by one of the ubiquitous scorpions or something much worse, since I had gone into a kind of war dance—which sent Nona fleeing to Achi for protection—still clutching my glasses. With these once more perched firmly on my nose, we returned to our camp, having agreed that we really didn't care about kangaroos. Besides, Nona had earned a celebration. Possibly she thought us both quite balmy, but I have always had an uncanny feeling that she fully comprehended the whole business.

It was several days later that Achi and I were lying about after dinner—the only possible position following the truly fierce *nasi goreng* Achi had concocted and of which we both ate far too much—and I hauled out my by now somewhat derelict copy of Wallace's book to see what more he might have to say about the Aru Islands. I started reading aloud, slowly so that Achi could interrupt if any words were unfamiliar to him, and came to a truly shattering statement (the one I deleted from my earlier quotation [page 176]): "Although I had been for months confined to the house by illness, and had lost much time by the want of the means of locomotion, and by missing the right season at the right place, I brought away with me more than nine thousand specimens of natural objects, of about sixteen hundred distinct species."

I was quiet for a very long time, and Achi said nothing, sensing, as he told me later, that I "had need of silence," while I nursed what was for me real despair. I had been so very proud of my collecting, which for the Aru Islands numbered (with Nona's help!) nearly two hundred specimens of insects of about forty species.

Now, I had known intellectually that Wallace had spent years in the East Indies, had had a variety of helpers, and considerable experience, but I had never truly assimilated all this factual information and, with all the enthusiasm and ignorance of youth, had bounded off to "complete the job he started." The arrogance of this attitude dismays me now, but it had been then nearly seventy-five years since Wallace had traveled the East Indies, and I was aware of the strides that had been made in so many fields, including natural history, and somehow assumed that with this up-to-date knowledge—of which I had in fact very little—I could certainly do better than even a genius who flourished in the middle of the last century. Obviously, as I began to realize that night, this was not the case.

Achi regarded me thoughtfully for a while and then said quietly, "Tuan, you are thinking that you have done no good in your collections?"

I nodded, and he went on.

"But, tuan, you are not here so long as Wallace, and we do not take birds. And is it not good that you show if some of the insects we catch are the same as his and some not?"

This cheered me somewhat and, though I do not believe he was thinking specifically of evolution, I proceeded to explain this to him in the most detailed terms, only to note that he looked less and less convinced as I went on.

"But, tuan, we catch very many insects that look like different things—twigs, leaves, even other animals; how do they know to look like twigs?"

With all the vast superiority of the white man, I announced that "They don't 'know' it, Achi, but ones that look like twigs are more likely to survive and have babies, and, moreover, babies that look like them. So finally, the ones like twigs or whatever it is are the only ones that survive."

"But why," said he, "do they start to look like twigs?"

There he had me, and, dear reader, he still has me. Some of the alleged facets of evolution I will swallow whole, but others—and in particular, some of the incredible and bizarre adaptations that crop up not only (though especially) in insects but in other animals as well —I find difficult to assign to "natural selection." It is quite one thing to point out that a white rabbit has little chance of living long enough to breed, while his brownish brother blends in with his surroundings, being furnished with natural camouflage, and stands a reasonable chance. But some of the utterly outlandish insects I did collect suggest that perhaps there is more to evolution than is generally recognized. Don't ask me what it is, because I don't know; but it was Achi who first caused me to query this process. I will not fall back on "God did it" —I have over the years been informed by some of my readers that "there is no mystery about this and such; it was God's will," or whatever. This may be so, but I still want to know *how* it was done—and why.

We talked long into the night, solving nothing, of

course, but by the time we turned in, I had forgotten my despair and had a renewed resolve to continue my vastly important work!

The next morning I arose with renewed confidence, though perhaps a niggling doubt in the back of my mind, and announced that we should set out in a direction we had not really explored before. We therefore headed north, paralleling the bank of the creek down which we had come to our present camp, with butterfly nets at the ready, and made a rather respectable collection of various kinds of insects. Nona, with her usual uncanny perspicacity, outdid herself—and gorged herself on the extra specimens.

I spent many hours carefully packing our specimens in the various containers that had been prepared for them and stowed them away in a large tin to be shipped back to the British Museum as soon as I reached "civilization," certain that however feeble my efforts, they did have value. The bearers and guides arrived, astonishingly, on schedule, and once again we headed for the coast, where a boat could be expected within a few days.

The trek back to the coast was relatively uneventful, though there was a minor crisis as we rounded a bend and inadvertently cornered a cassowary. Young cassowaries are kept as pets by many of the natives, being allowed to run about like domestic fowl. The young are striped brown and black and look quite different from the mature birds with their bristlelike dark body plumage, large bony helmet or casque, and garishly colored neck and, in most species, wattles. The Aru Islanders I met did not keep the mature birds, as is done in some places, the wretched creatures being placed in cages hardly larger than the birds themselves. The plumes are much valued, and the casques are also used for ornaments, but the grown bird can be frightfully dangerous. Ordinarily they are shy and retiring and would rather run than fight, but when cornered they attack by leaping at you feet first. The middle toe is armed with a long, straight, murderous nail that can slice off an arm or disembowel a man with ease, and many a native has been killed in just this way. Fortunately, in our case we had room to maneuver, and everybody ran, thus giving the cassowary an unimpeded path back into his part of the forest. He took immediate advantage of this and charged off, head down, straight through the tangled vegetation, thorns and all, at what seemed to me incredible speed. I was told later that they can run at speeds up to thirty miles an hour, and simply go over or under anything they can't go through, even swimming (and the sight they present then must be appalling). They are flightless, of course, and the various species range from four to five feet in height, the females being larger than the males and just as deadly.

Our safari having reassembled, we proceeded without further difficulty back to their little village. They assured me that ordinarily they do not run from cassowaries but had not been armed for such an encounter and also had not wished to risk damage to my baggage. Inasmuch as this had been flung in a variety of directions at the moment of crisis, I tended to discount the second half of their explanation but nevertheless expressed myself as deeply touched by their concern for my belongings. As soon as we could do so tactfully, Achi and I carried out an inventory but found "all present and correct."

Two days later I was delighted to see one of the spanking-clean little Dutch launches dropping anchor, and I promptly sought the captain, who readily agreed to take us as passengers. He was going straight on to Macassar rather than stopping at Ceram, which I saw only as a dim blur on the horizon. I should have liked to have visited Ceram, which also has some unique animals, but the captain, though sympathetic, was unable to revise his schedule.

I went back to the same hotel I had stayed in before in Macassar and ate a splendid dinner of an omelette with asparagus and chicken with rice and fell into bed. I awoke rather late the next morning, having slept in my dressing gown as my orange pyjamas (the envy of the native staff) were being washed, and had a cup of coffee in the comfortable full-length chair on the verandah before my room. After breakfast I continued to lounge about, having given Achi carte blanche to go and do as he pleased for a day or two. I was happily contemplating visits to some of the brighter night spots and temporary release from the duties incumbent on a naturalist when I became aware of a small procession headed in my direction. The staff, remembering my peculiar behavior on my previous visit, had gone to work on my behalf and now presented me with a number of beetles, including one very interesting Lamellicorn [Stag] Beetle and a good moth. Naturally, I could not turn these down and so had to go right back to work. The most touching—and quite useless—tribute came from a miniscule person who, beaming from ear to ear, brought me a lamp globe filled with dessicated parts of insects.

They filled a twelve-inch box (which I later dumped) and made him terribly proud.

Partly in self-defense, I suddenly decided to visit the "falls" and found that Willy, an Alsatian and the director of the hotel, and an American chap were keen to go too, and that Willy would provide a car. Our departure was comic, the comedy being provided by three bottles of violently colored lemonade, sandwiches, glasses, topees, bug net and bag, and my best trousers. We dashed about Macassar on several errands and then stopped at the hotel again, where more lemonade was taken aboard, while I put on my second-best trousers. We then got under way, driving along a very fine new road to the north of the town. The scenery was at first coconut palm and kampong and later vast paddy fields bounded on the horizon by an apparently unbroken line of trees. This later gave way to a very queer level "veldt" of smooth, lawnlike grass and billowing clumps of thorn bush and evergreen trees. There were absolutely no houses, but hundreds of gray-and-pink buffalo grazing unattended or wallowing in small-sized mud baths of a glutinous consistency and apparently deep. We then came unexpectedly to Maros, a diminutive but active town with a perfectly vast *pasar* [market] (a number of rectangular, low concrete platforms variously roofed and standing behind a low bamboo fence) and desporting a neat flower-bedecked European quarter inhabited by ten whites. It has a river, large, muddy, and apt to misbehave itself; a rough but doubtless efficient embankment marked where it had decanted itself into the town the previous year to the discomfort of many Arab shopkeepers and gentlemen of the Orient who had no rooftops or upper floors to retreat to.

The country after this flourishing burg was for the most part paddy fields, equally vast and green, with a row of low native houses built on piles and filled with swarthy idle men and women, bordering the road on one side. Suddenly, a vast, rounded rock appeared on the left-hand side of the road, covered with dense scrub and dropping unconformably into the paddy fields. We were now approaching the long line of beautiful gray-blue hills, when the approach seemed suddenly to stop, and we found ourselves at the foot of a 200-foot wall of loose, porous, cave-riddled coralline limestone covered with dense vegetation and rising at an angle of 90 degrees from the paddy fields. The shape (probably due to excessive and quick erosion of a once-level raised plateau) of these foothills was exotic in the extreme, i.e., a succession of rounded, knoblike humps, sometimes even bulbous. Clefts some 40 feet wide reached from the top to the very level of the plain, and their edge abutted and receded like an erratic ocean-bound seacoast.

The road followed a narrow canal constructed to carry water to the paddy fields and ran beneath a continuous archway of tamarind trees, delicate of foliage and dark of trunk. We left the road and plunged into a narrow cul-de-sac in the hills by a rough track. The weird cliffs, from which streams and rivers bubbled and huge earthen stalactites hung, closed in on us, and we stopped at a roofed platform adjoined by a row of permanent concrete bathing cubicles. Getting out of the car, we walked further along a path of large, irregular stones by a muddy, swirling, madly rushing river. At this point the path went under the cliff by a natural undercut, from the roof of which water dripped in a kind of shower onto a soft, sandy floor, while the cliff towered for hundreds of feet above, with thick, stunted vegetation clinging to it, as if it were a piece of the world tilted to an angle of 120 degrees.

Turning a bend, we arrived at a little Japanese-looking shelter much eaten by white ants and enveloped in spray from a wonderful low waterfall where a vast volume of water was cast up into a rushing parabola by a huge boulder in its course. There was a flight of wooden steps at the edge of the stream by which persons could ascend to the river above and take a pleasant walk to the lake that feeds it, but these were partly obscured by the excess of water. One could stand for hours watching those condensed waters hurrying by as if eager to get away from the catapult that had cast them from the gorge, but my roving eye had spotted several species of gorgeous *Papilio* butterfly "lapping" about, so I sent the driver back for my bag and began stalking these as they sucked at the wet mud, rolling from side to side in the peculiar manner common to large tropical butterflies. I was very lucky in securing several by wild strokes in the air, reminiscent of the racquets court, while Willy stood by holding the box. After a bit, I handed the net over to the crowd of mirthful native onlookers, and we retired to devour planklike sandwiches and flame-colored lemonade (manufactured by a retired Armenian ship's engineer in Soerabaja to satisfy the colorful mind of the natives) under the roof shelter. After this repast we sat and discussed religion and Persian politics, while the natives brought me several rare *Papilios* in beautiful condition.

When we got back into the car, I picked up a puppy (which had been taking the rough edge off my sandwiches) and began to pet it, which very much puzzled and rather disgusted the natives, who are very much averse to handling dogs and never think of showing them unnecessary kindness. We arrived back at about 4:15 P.M. after passing several parties of unknown white people in "freight cars" (i.e., taxis) and stopping once to secure a flying lizard that had unwisely chosen the back seat of the car as its alighting place.

I just had tea and then descended to view the crowd of travelers (American and Australian) who had arrived on a boat from Sydney. I then walked along to a bookshop but found nothing to interest me and so boarded a taxi, telling the driver to cruise around slowly. We kept as near the coast to the south of the town as we could, and, feeling in a mad mood, I waved and yelled from the back of the open car to all the cheerful little people who smiled and called to me, such a strange sight—a young man driving about the town at eventide without a girl. The cheery little taximan asked me if I wanted a lady to drive around with, which I did, but knowing the time to be short—I had still to arrange our passage on a boat that was going on to Java and Sumatra—I contented myself with returning the professional "glad eyes" turned upon me and returned to the hotel rather early.

After transacting the necessary business I rounded up Achi and told him to be ready to sail the next day and to see to the heavy baggage that had been following us around. I then had dinner, wrote in my diary until quite late, and finally fell into bed.

Willy wakened me the next afternoon, announcing breathlessly that it was three thirty and that I could not catch my boat. After leaping from bed I discovered that he had a "sense of humor"—it was only one thirty—and so dressed rather more slowly and had a very bad lunch. I then fell wholeheartedly to packing, and while I was still in the throes of same, the shipping agent arrived. I was in an idiotic mood, and my methods of packing much amused this gentleman. However, after a fine display of obscene language and unpublishable rhetoric, I got everything battened down, and we descended to the lounge. I paid my bill, which was not ruinous, and then Willy got my luggage down, while we sat placidly talking eight minutes before the boat was due to sail. We arrived, however, with time to spare, disentangled an unhappy-looking Achi from a sea of red tape involving our heavy baggage, and the four of us went on board.

The boat was literally full—I can say no more for it— the decks (all three) being crammed with a voluble crowd of bright-eyed half-castes, squawking, straw-haired Dutch children in something like overalls, pursued by pretty little native babus, and a lot of men, great in volume if nothing else and representative of every company in Macassar, making this event an excuse for unlimited beer drinking in the shortest possible time. Willy and the agent got me into my cabin, and we talked until they had to go ashore. Mournful community singing, whether due to alcohol or Christianity I was unable to ascertain, began above, and then an army of brown humans in European dress, bordering on beauty among the so-called weaker sex, poured down the companionway onto the quay, where they formed a closely packed phalanx, vaguely grinning and staring at a point above our deck. After the loosing of many ropes, the breaking of others, and a pull by a lighter, we got clear and moved slowly out.

I had been given a pamphlet on Macassar written by a sometime "divine" from Melbourne in which he gives a completely erroneous impression of native life among the Bugis. If a man considers tables and bedroom furniture necessary, practicable, or even comfortable in an *atap* house, let him not tell people in Australia that the natives are "a wretched, pitilessly poor, terrified race, nearer animals than men," for they are a far more cheery, contented, humorous, bold, and flirtatious-minded crowd than the Australians.

❧ 15 ❧

Southwest Sumatra and the Cloud Forest:
Tube-Nosed Fruit Bats, Sun Bears,
Tarsiers, and a Binturong;
The Mentawi Islands

LATE THE NEXT AFTERNOON
I went on deck and watched our slow entry into Boeleleng, Bali, a place I had not expected to revisit. I
wished to go ashore with a lot of passengers who were
getting off, but we were only staying an hour, the clocks
had to be put back twenty minutes, and it takes roughly
fifteen minutes to get ashore, so I had to content myself
with watching the lighters come alongside, waving to
Phatima, who was in a rowboat, and observing this
beautiful little garden island shimmering beneath a
cloudless steel-blue sky. There is a narrow coastal plain
covered with palms, and behind this rise thickly wooded,
majestically shaped mountains, slashed by deep ravines
that make the bands of light and shade contrast star-
tlingly.

We discharged a little cargo, and a native alone in a huge prau asked me to catch his rope and make it fast, as there were no sailors nearby; this I did in the true nautical style, which very much surprised him. Just before the boat sailed, when many passengers came on, Phatima arrived and delayed our sailing for some twenty minutes selling her silver goods.

This boat was going on to Ceylon and India, and instead of the usual route up the east coast of Java and then Sumatra, it maneuvered through the Bali Strait and proceeded up the western coasts of those islands, stopping in Sumatra only at Padang, where I disembarked.

Sumatra as a whole is odd in several respects—it is enormous,* densely forested, and comparatively uninhabited—and for the zoologist it is, together with the tip of Malaya and a few neighboring islands, nearly unique. Many animals of the Asiatic mainland are found here, but many others are truly relic animals found nowhere else. The tapirs we had seen on our way to Achi's village are among these latter; their only near relatives are the New World Tapirs, of which there are three species, though all four species constitute a single genus. The Barisan Mountains, from Mount Marapi a bit north of Padang, all along the coast down to the southern tip of Sumatra, are in many ways even odder than the rest of Sumatra and form a quite separate ecological area. Despite the fact that they run right into the Boekits Mountains which

---

*It is the sixth largest island, ranking behind Greenland, New Guinea, Borneo, Madagascar, and Baffin Island, with an area of 164,165 square miles (i.e., larger than the state of California).

bisect northern Sumatra, there is a distinct break between them and the Boekits but, on the other hand, a link with the really extraordinary Mentawi Islands about fifty miles off shore.

I wanted very much to get into the Barisan Mountains, but this was really impossible without a full-scale "expedition," for which I had neither the time nor the money. There were no guides available, and the official I asked for information was completely scandalized at the idea of my attempting to go in on my own. He pointed out that the terrain and vegetation were such that I would soon get lost, with no hope of being found, if I did not fall into a ravine and break my neck first. Undeterred, I gave him a lengthy (and somewhat exaggerated) account of my travels in the East Indies and my prowess in finding my way out of jungles, and attributed to Achi abilities that would have astonished that modest person. The best I got from all this was a reluctant statement that he would think about it and that I should come to see him again tomorrow.

Achi and I wandered around Padang that evening, chumbling about the possibility of sneaking off, though this was unlikely to be feasible. It is not easy for a European to make himself inconspicuous among the Malays, particularly if he is six feet tall, and I had the distinct feeling that the hotel staff had been told to report my comings and goings, especially the latter. Furthermore, Achi was not happy about trying to circumvent official dictums, though he had become as enthusiastic an "explorer" and collector as I was, and he counseled patience. Patience was not one of my virtues, but I did my best to control myself, and Achi led me to a small market-place where birds and other animals were for sale, thinking this might at least distract me for the moment.

For the most part the mammals were those already known to me, but I was intrigued by one that I later identified as having been a Hemigale, or Hardwicke's Palm-Civet *(Hemigalus hardwickii)* [see Figure 32]. These beautiful animals are sometimes seen in zoos but little is known of them. Presumably they feed on birds and other small animals and climb trees like other species of Palm-Civet; but the hair on the back of the neck goes forward instead of backward as it does in all ordinary animals, including ourselves, and the pattern of its coat is peculiar. The owner did not seem to like me and would not sell it to me, even with Achi's intervention. The birds were of every variety, including some Birds of Paradise of various species, but I did not, of course, collect birds and so was not interested in buying any.

I returned to the government offices the next morning, only to be told that the *tuan besar* had been called away for the day and had left word that I should come again at ten the next morning. Thus frustrated, I spent the day writing up my diary, visiting the post office, various banks, shipping offices, and the like, and in making plans for my journey home, convinced that the mysterious mountains that met my gaze would be barred to me. I was growing rather short of cash, and I was still far from the halfway point at which further funds would be forthcoming. A careful calculation indicated that with judicious expenditure I could be certain of getting to Singapore—and no further. Achi had become very casual indeed about being actually paid his admittedly small salary, but I was honor-bound to pay him the full sum owed him, and this left me with not a great deal over. It also left me more depressed than ever.

Achi came in just as I slammed my accounts book shut and suggested that we should go to a place on the outskirts of the town where he had been told there were "many bats." So we went, and with remarkable originality for me, I managed to bring down a Tube-Nosed Fruit Bat. This is a most disconcerting animal, and I here resort to drawings [see Figures 29 and 30]. This bat is also known as the Harpy Bat, but Tube-Nosed is a better description, though no one, so far as I know, has ever determined why it needs nostrils drawn out into a couple of pieces of flexible tubing. Fruit-Bats do feed hanging upside down, and I once watched some other species of fruit-eating bat doing just this. They took the loose fruit between their wings, seizing it with their two clawed thumbs, which are on the edge of the wings. These greedy little beasts were eating ripe guavas, and they gobbled so fast that all the sticky juice poured out of the corners of their mouths (which were above their noses because they were upside down) and trickled into their nostrils. Every now and then they had to stop eating to cough, splutter, and sneeze as their nostrils became filled up with the liquid. The Harpy's "tubes" would prevent this and carry the wasted juice away so that it could drip free of their breathing apparatus. The unfortunate thing about this nice theory is that the stomachs of the Tube-Nosed Fruit-Bats are found to be full of beetles and flies, showing that they are predominantly insect eaters!

There are several kinds of Harpy found in the islands of Indonesia and the western Pacific—Celebes, New

Guinea, New Ireland, and the Solomon Islands—and in the very northernmost part of Australia. They are all light fawn, ashy, buff, or even cream colored. Many have a dark stripe running down their spines, and all have sharply marked yellow spots on the wings and the naked parts of their limbs. Their mouths are surrounded by a single line of little naked pimples, and they have only twenty-four teeth (we have thirty-two, most mammals forty-four). Practically nothing is known of their habits.

I spent several unhappy hours preparing this monstrosity but finally got it properly done up and packed with all the other specimens I had collected and had not yet sent on. This packet I sealed carefully and took to a shipping agent the first thing next morning. I then headed once more for the government agent.

He sat and stared at me for what seemed a long time, but finally spoke.

"Mijnheer Sanderson. You can go if you go exactly where I tell you, and do not go out of this place I send you. Yesterday I talked with a man in a small village— why he lives there I do not know; he could live here more comfortably—and there is a ravine that goes up the mountain from close to his house. If you will not leave that ravine but only stay in it, then I will permit. Otherwise—but you are an English gentleman and I will take your word."

I was not an English gentleman; I was and remained a Scot; but on this occasion I swallowed my pride, feeling that this was hardly the time to argue the point,* and

---

*It would seem to me to be unnecessary to explain this, but many people apparently do not understand why the Scots object

gave him my word. Considering the place he sent us, I wondered later why he bothered to ask for my word. Escape from that "ravine" was hardly possible.

The village was south of Padang, and small boats plied up and down the coast regularly (for all practical purposes there weren't any roads). Achi and I chose and packed our gear with exceptional care, and we came up with a quite manageable set of bags. We found a willing ferryman and stowed our things for the short trip, which was accomplished without incident, though the chap who took us spent his time cheerfully predicting all sorts of dire events certain to befall us in the mountains. I hoped fervently that he was wrong; otherwise we were in for a rather parroty time of it.

In due course he landed us on a somewhat rickety-looking pier, and after asking directions and finding a man with a small cart to take our bags, we found the gentleman who would direct us to the ravine in which we would be permitted to lose ourselves. I had with me a letter of introduction, but he hardly glanced at it and seemed to know what I was up to. He advised waiting until the next morning before setting out, and drew me a "map," a word I use advisedly, since it consisted primarily of broken lines to indicate that he *thought* it went thataway just about there but wasn't sure! About the only thing he was sure of was that it began about a

---

to being called English. Experience indicates that this is made clear by asking a U.S. citizen whether he would mind being called Canadian; the invariable response is, "But I'm not Canadian." Well, the Scots aren't English. Their country is part of Great Britain. So is England, which is occupied by the English. [S. W. S.]

mile from his house. He had been into it a short distance and told me that its general direction was more or less straight up and that I would find the vegetation "difficult," but that there was a watercourse we could follow. As long as we stayed within reach of this, we should be all right and could always follow it out of the ravine. His map proved wholly inaccurate, but he was right about the "straight up"—it was so "straight up" that occasionally the watercourse was beneath rather than beside us!

At first light the next morning we had a very hearty breakfast, beginning with some really excellent porridge and going on through the eggs-and-bacon bit, topping it off with delicious fruits. My inclination afterward was to sit peacefully and let it digest, but my host was displaying signs of agitation and insisted that we start at once. We therefore loaded our packs and set out along a neatly trimmed path through his garden, passed through a gate in the bamboo fence that surrounded his property, and found ourselves against a wall of vegetation. Now, I had thought that the forests we had visited before had been "jungle," and so they had been, but this was more so.

The "ordinary" jungles I had been in had seemed lush to me, but this was an edge of a really rain-soaked forest, which makes other jungle look positively barren by comparison. We had first to cut and crawl our way through a tangled mass of herbs, shrubs, and small trees entwined by vines and covered with parasitic plants of all description, and all dripping water still though the rain had stopped an hour before. It took us nearly an hour to penetrate this massed vegetation, and often we found it easier to snake our way along the ground, hauling our bags behind us and constantly having to yank them and ourselves free of thorns or twisting vines that seemed intent on preventing our passage. I don't know how thick this "wall" was; it was what most people envision when they think of the jungle, and results from "excessive" sunlight and, in cases such as this, from rainfall that measures up to two hundred inches a year.*

Once through this tangle we emerged into a columned cathedral of green and gray, moister than the jungles I had seen before and somehow dimmer, in part because the steep walls of the canyon—for this is what it was— blocked what little light there might have been. The jungle giants grew on its steep walls, their crowns meeting across a jumbled mass of boulders over which poured a network of tiny streams, broken here and there by diminutive waterfalls. We climbed ever upward, clinging now to roots, now to vines, and again to fragile handholds in the rocks. Gradually the giants were left below us, and trees of more modest height took their place. Too, a few palms appeared, and giant tree ferns twice and more my height. And then we seemed to cross some natural barrier. I felt as if I had entered some other universe, dimly lit, eerily green, filled with the hums and buzzes of insects, the cries of innumerable birds, the constant drip of water. We had reached the cloud forest. Here the sun was held at bay, and the fogs never dissipated, and we walked on a carpet of moss that oozed moisture at every step, while as far as the eye could see, every surface—trees, boulders, even leaves—was cov-

---

*Rainfall along Sumatra's east coast averages 80 to 120 inches a year; on the southwest, 120 to 200 inches, even more concentrated here because the mountains come right down to the coast. [S. W. S.]

ered with moss and ferns, lichens and parasitic plants. Not only terror but beauty can send a shiver down the spine, and I confess I wept.

Whether it was truly practical matters or whether it was that I felt that if I stayed here I should never consent to leave I am not sure even now, but we made our way back, halfway down the walls of the canyon. Here we stopped for a very late lunch and then started to go on again. The air was very still but seemed to shimmer, and suddenly I felt rather dizzy. Things seemed to wave about a bit and the ground to feel unsteady under my feet. What I can only describe as a pulsation passed beneath us, and I grabbed a nearby vine for support, hanging on for some minutes as the pulsations continued. Then all was still again. I looked at Achi to see if I was imagining things, but he nodded brightly and said, "Small earthquake, tuan." Now of course I knew that this whole area is subject to earthquakes as well as volcanic activity, and I had been aware of minor temblors elsewhere—the kind that rattle the dishes a bit— but had not experienced one while in a forest. It seemed to have no effect at all, but later I learned that it was indeed a "small" earthquake. A severe one does shift the ground about, but (and later experience tends to confirm this), barring destruction of a particular "square" of ground, the trees thereon do not fall; they simply go up and down, being tightly woven together by the various vines that grow through the canopy.

Taking a deep breath and hoping there would be no further quakes, we clambered up along the moss-covered boulders that bordered the other side of the gorge and came after a time to an almost circular dell of indescribable beauty. Tiny plants provided a soft carpet underfoot, while the great trunks and buttress roots formed a near stockade around us. We made our camp here, clearing a tiny patch of ground in the angle of two roots for a fire and draping the light tarpaulin over the lower end of these as a shelter. Leaning against the roots, we could look straight up perhaps a hundred feet to the greenery that formed the canopy, decked with masses of smaller plants, the parasites that cling to all tropical trees, and dangling with a multitude of vines. Butterflies fluttered about the clearing, while tiny flies hovered in a single shaft of sunlight that filtered between the far-off leaves above.

Once established, we set out to explore the vicinity of our camp, whacking notches in the great trees to enable us to find our way back. We found a tiny rivulet that led back toward the main stream and followed this for a way, coming to a small sandy bank covered with tracks of birds and mammals. Achi pointed out one set of tracks that were clearly those of a cat. We never saw any other trace of their maker, and since there are several small cats to be found in that area,* I could not say which it might have been. Little is known of any of these, and I was content at the time to note that the tracks were very small and therefore not those of a leopard that might leap out at me when I was least expecting it, though I would have dearly loved to have seen a Clouded Leopard (*Profelis nebulosa*). These beautiful animals are intermediate in

---

*These seem to include the Leopard-Cat (*Felis bengalensis*); Plain Cats (*F. planiceps*)—so-called because they have unmarked coats, unlike other cats; the Marbled Cat (*F. marmorata*); and the Bay-Cat (*F. aurata*). [S. W. S.]

size between the great cats (lions, tigers, et al.) and the ocelots and their ilk. The ground color of the coat is a light buff, marked with large cloudlike black patches, and they have exceptionally long tails. They are rather rare even in the wilderness of southern Sumatra, but tend to lurk near villages. Reportedly the natives do not fear them, though they don't like having them around, since they apparently show a distinct liking for poultry. They sleep in trees and also are said to lie in wait for their prey on low branches, dropping on their victims as they pass beneath. The other, smaller cats are equally hard to find or see, being solitary, neatly camouflaged, and wary. In fact, in many years of collecting I rarely saw any of the cats. On the plains of Africa, of course, lions are practically verminous, which gives the movie-going public a very erroneous idea of the habits and "visibility" of the cats generally. Except for the tiger, I never saw any on this trip.

With the usual malice aforethought, I sent Achi back to bring me a half dozen traps, which I carefully laid near this sand bank. I relaid them daily, and daily found them sprung by some four-footed genius, but never caught anything in them. It was very depressing.

Several days after our arrival I had finished laying another line of traps farther up the gorge and was lying in wait for a particularly beautiful butterfly that refused to come out into the open where I could secure it without damaging its wings, when I became increasingly aware of the sensation of being watched. Knowing Achi to be elsewhere, this made me quite nervous, and I turned round rather suddenly. Standing there observing me was a curious but not unfriendly Sun-Bear *(Helarctos)*. These animals are not very large as bears go, the largest measuring only some four and a half feet in length, but they look much larger when standing on their hind legs, which they seem to do rather often. They have a roughly crescent-shaped light patch on the chest and a pale "face," with a rather benign expression (for a bear at any rate). My first and very fleeting impression was that I was being peered at by an extremely hairy and massive "native," but the second half of my "double take" revealed the nature of the beast, and I retreated, bowing quite idiotically. He followed me for a few steps—on his hind legs at that—and then dropped to all fours and went his own way. This was not my only encounter with these bears, but the initial effect was always the same. In the dim light of the forest I invariably mistook them for people at first glance (they always sneaked up behind me anyway), though a photograph taken in a zoo will undoubtedly make you wonder why.

Squirrels also eluded me. Whether there was something about the light in this forest or whether my shooting had simply deteriorated, I do not know, but though I saw many squirrels, some of them giant types, I never managed to collect any.

I decided to do something I had not done before. This was to go out at night to do some collecting. Many animals are nocturnal and sleep all day, curled up in holes in tree trunks or elsewhere, and though I had wandered about at dawn—I seem to have been an awfully early riser in those days—and at dusk and had seen animals that are not visible during daylight hours, I had never been out during those hours when the truly nocturnal animals come forth.

Going out at night posed a major problem, since I had no flashlight and dared not stumble about in the darkness. I had no idea what we might run into, either animate or inanimate (in the form of tree roots or potholes), and there was always the minor problem of getting lost in the maze of giant trunks that made up the forest. Achi went into what is usually called a "brown study" and then disappeared. I could hear the occasional clang of the machete as he marked his trail, and I became somewhat confused as the sound rang out from a seemingly unlimited number of directions and I began to wonder how many Achis there were banging about the jungle. The sounds, however, eventually settled down in one direction and finally became consistently louder as Achi made his way back. He appeared with a bunch of odd-looking slender leaves and laid these on a makeshift grill over the now dull embers of our fire. After a while he pronounced them "cured" and tied them to a slender piece of sapling. He then built up the fire and produced dinner.

After we had eaten, we sat down (figuratively speaking) and discussed what we might need or ought to take with us. I was somewhat wary of the whole exercise by this time, being convinced that we would get lost or worse, but was unwilling to admit that I was getting cold feet and so went about collecting the necessary equipment. I was none too sanguine about Achi's torch, either, expecting it to give out about one hundred yards from camp. I don't know what species the leaves were, but they burned for nearly four hours, and we were within sight of the glow of our campfire before they finally sputtered out.

We waited until it was truly dark and the night noises had started in earnest, and then Achi lit his torch and we sallied forth to see what might be seen. There were rustlings far above us and small sounds all around, but at first we saw nothing. Then, as Achi held the torch aloft, a myriad of eyes became visible. Many of these were spiders whose multifaceted eyes reflected our light, but one pair of eyes like saucers shone from a sapling growing at the edge of a grove of small trees. At first I could not make out the owner of the eyes, but as I grew accustomed to the play of light and shadow in this otherwise black world, I realized that these belonged to a tarsier.

These little rat-sized sprites have soft woolly fur, long tails, huge eyes, and large hands and feet, with long slim fingers and toes terminating in huge clinging pads like those of tree frogs [see Figure 31]. In habits they are also surprisingly like tree frogs, leaping about dense foliage, catching insects. There are a dozen kinds of Tarsiers, ordinarily grouped into three species, a Philippine form (*Tarsius syrichta*), a Bornean-Sumatran (*T. bancanus*), and a Celebesean (*T. spectrum*), and found in strictly limited areas. I had not seen any in Celebes, but there they are known only from a small area in the center of the main island, and I had not reached this spot. All the Tarsiers represent the last remaining twig of a previously sturdy branch of primate stock that sprouted off the main trunk at least as long ago as sixty million years, in what is called the Palaeocene Period. The earliest were American, and North American at that, though they are now limited to the Philippines and some of the Indonesian islands. They are classed with the monkeys, apes, and ourselves rather than with the lemurs, the lorisoids, and the tupaioids, or tree shrews, our "ultimate ancestors." Actually, they have more anatomical features in common with the lemurs of Madagascar, but their noses are simple like ours, and they don't really belong with the lower primates, an abstruse matter I don't intend to discuss further here!

I was frankly thrilled to see this tiny creature, and we watched it for some time. While the light illuminated it, it did nothing, being apparently dazed by the unaccustomed light, but the moment Achi lowered the light behind a large tree trunk, the tarsier simply vanished. We tried to see where it had gone but soon gave up.

We saw nothing else of note that night or the next, but on the third night we did bump into something, though it was only after peering at it for some time that we agreed that we were seeing what we thought we saw. This was that most improbable animal, the Binturong (*Arctictis*), which in the wild is a dark green color (though actually a grizzled gray), probably due to some kind of algal growth, and hence almost perfectly camouflaged. It is related to the civets but looks more bearlike than anything else. Its tail, however, is rather long and heavily furred with coarse hair like the rest of its body—and is prehensile. This last has always struck me as being positively "illegal." No animal of this size and that looks like this should have a prehensile tail, but it does. It trundles along like a bear, walking on the whole foot rather than mincing along on its toes as do the other civets. The ears bear large, drooping tufts of hair that give it a terribly forlorn look. This was apparently a young one, measuring perhaps four feet including the tail. Adults may reach six feet.

It trundled about on a large tree that hung out at an angle over the edge of a small cliff, making little rumbling, growling noises as it searched for food, and seemed undisturbed by our torch, but shortly moved off into what was for us unknown territory, and we dared not try to follow.

It was soon clear that if we wished really to see animals at night, we would have to combine our torchlight expeditions with tree climbing, and this I was not prepared to do. Whenever we stood still, and particularly if we shielded the torch, a positive cacaphony of sound broke out above us, and it was plain that the canopy was alive with animals. By chance, we must have been under a major "highway," since later experience showed that so much traffic is unusual, but it was frustrating in the extreme to hear so much going on, or past, and not be able to see anything. The light from our torch did not truly carry to the canopy, though the lowest leaves were dimly visible. Of course, there were scufflings on the ground, and mousy creatures flitted back and forth collecting seeds that had dropped from the trees above, but vanished as soon as we moved. I had not then learned the trick of "drifting" among animals, a method that permits you to move among them without causing alarm. Here we tried to change our vantage point by moving from one spot to another as quickly as possible, managing only to terrify everything in the area. We had then to sit very still for a time until the less wary again poked their noses out.

There were bats in plenty, diving and twisting after insects in the torchlight, but I would not have dared to use the shotgun in these circumstances, being uncertain just what the scatter pattern was and whether it might include Achi in the process. These were small bats, but apart from being obviously insect eaters, I could not identify them. Some bats are readily identifiable at a distance, but others have to be examined closely, since species differences depend on such things as the construction of the ears!

My allotted period in the canyon having run out, we made our way slowly down and finally cut our way back through the edge of the jungle, arriving just in time for tea, though my host seemed to be indulging in something more akin to Irish coffee. He had had rather a lot of it, in fact, and was somewhat the worse for wear. Just as soon as I could tactfully do so, I withdrew and consulted with Achi, who proved to have received a rather odd welcome himself. I therefore determined not to stay there the night and went in search of a hotel, but before I had properly started on this endeavor, I was approached by a beaming gentleman whose racial heritage was indefinable; he appeared to have something of every race and subrace known, plus perhaps a dash of Proboscis Monkey thrown in, but the overall effect was, astonishingly enough, not unpleasing.

My fame as a "mad Englishman" had apparently preceded me, for he informed me that he had a boat and was leaving for the Mentawi Islands and surely I would want to go. I did, but despite a prolonged conversation in English, kitchen Malay (at which I was now fairly fluent), French, and a tiny smattering of Hollands, I could not find out how much he wanted or how long he was going to be there, since I would apparently be dependent on him for the return trip also. Achi hove in sight and took over the negotiations. These were completed in due course, Achi having come up with some other language I didn't know he knew. The price asked was ridiculous, something like one rupiah [guilder*] round trip, but the catch was that he would be returning the next evening. This, of course, left almost no time for a visit, but at that price I couldn't resist. It also gave me a splendid reason for declining to stay the night with my erstwhile host. When I returned to Penang, I learned that his benders were extremely infrequent but likely to be prolonged and sometimes rather violent. As it was, I'm not sure he noticed my departure!

The Mentawis are volcanic and surrounded by really very dangerous sunken coral reefs, and it occurred to me that it was perhaps not a good idea to sail for them at dusk, but the "captain" had no intention of losing his boat and hove to until full light as soon as he heard shoal water ahead. He was apparently using some kind of navigational method all his own, since he seemed to ignore currents, winds, and even stars, tacking back and forth for no discernible reason. Whatever his method, it worked, and he landed us safely on Siberoet Island, the northernmost of this little chain.

As a group these islands are most odd, and in addition, each is quite different from the next in climate, appearance, flora and fauna, though why this should be so has never been fully explained. There are several small rivers on Siberoet, and all the islands are heavily forested.

The natives are Caucasian in type and are believed to have preceded the Batuk peoples of Sumatra. They have

*About 25¢ [S. W. S.]

/ 227

golden-brown skin, black hair, and dark eyes, and like the Hawaiians they wear flowers in their hair or tucked behind the ears. They also go in for tattooing. Although formerly pirates, they showed no warlike tendencies and were most hospitable during my all too brief stay. I saw few signs of agriculture, and the Resident there told me they depend primarily on fishing and hunting.

I spent the day wandering about the native market and climbing nearby hills, collecting insects and keeping a keen watch in hopes of seeing some of the animals that are unique to these islands. Oddly enough, a number of animals are found on Siberoet and (at least) South Pagai, but not on Sipora which lies between them or even, apparently, North Pagai. One of these is the so-called Mentawi Islands Langur *(Simias concolor)*, which is technically a Snub-Nosed Monkey, though it is not much like any others of their genus either, except for their noses. It has very short hands and feet, with very long fingers and toes, and a tiny, slender, naked tail about six inches long. In truth they look more like macaques, of which the Rhesus Monkey is the best-known species. Here again, the typical form on Sumatra is *Macaca nemestrina nemestrina*, while the Mentawi Islands form is *Macaca nemestrina pagensis* and is quite distinct. The former, usually called Pigtailed Macaques, are trained, especially in Achin but also in other parts of Sumatra, to harvest coconuts and other such "unreachable" fruits. It is an experience to watch them. I once saw one that got its rope looped around limbs in such a way that it appeared to be hopelessly entangled, but it invariably unraveled itself by following the rope backward, weaving under and over limbs, until it was free to descend. Often it held the slack in its left hand, away from snags.

Another monkey, which I saw in the marketplace, is the Lutong *(Trachypithecus potenziani).* This is born a bright gold color, but adults are black above and golden orange below, with vivid white cheeks and throat. This one seemed to be someone's pet, but it did not encourage familiarities from strangers.

I hoped, rather irrationally to be sure, to see a Pigmy Siamang *(Brachytanities klossi* or *Symphalangus klossi,* depending on your authority), though these are found only on South Pagai Island and are uncommon even there. They were not even discovered until 1903. This is much smaller than the Siamang of Sumatra and has less webbing between the toes, but presumably much the same temperament. I never encountered a live one, but a zoologist I met some years later characterized them as "very nervous."

I arrived back at the pier with my pockets filled with butterflies in paper triangles and other insects in improvised packets of all sorts. With no time to do a proper packing job, I settled for getting them all into one bundle and slipping them into my biggest suitcase, wedging them between the folds of my very best suit. Achi and our boatman, wearing a smile of pure joy on his amiable face, arrived shortly, and we slipped past the reefs before dark.

The next day we anchored safely up the coast at Painan and then went on to Padang on one of the little coastal boats.

Now I really had a problem, because I had to get to

Singapore to catch a boat for the first lap of my home-ward journey. As the crow is alleged to fly, Singapore is less than three hundred miles from Padang. Practically, since I would not fly (if there was an airfield at Padang, which I don't remember), it was a great deal farther than that; I had to get back to Batavia [Djakarta] to find a mail packet or other steamer to make that trip. Hence I went to the local shipping office to make enquiries. The top chap was away, but a clerk who spoke fastidious English brought out a monumental pile of papers having to do with what boats went where and proceeded to run his immaculately groomed finger down seemingly unintelligible columns of figures and names. I had just about reached the conclusion that there were no more boats that year when the finger paused triumphantly, and he announced that there was a boat that would stop the next day. He was cagey about just what kind of a boat, but the estimated fare, which I should have to arrange with the captain, was more than reasonable, and I dared not chance waiting for another boat in any case.

It proved to be little more than a barge, but it did deposit us at Soerabaya, where I could easily get a boat for Singapore via Batavia. Going through customs was a lengthy process, since I had now to be certain that all my other baggage had caught up with me, but various clerks checked carefully and found that all but one were being held in bond.* To my everlasting chagrin, the missing case contained my specimens from the Aru Islands. It

---

*So far as I can determine, everything had been shipped here to be looked after by the shipping firm run by "the famous Pat Lawrence," whoever he was—Ivan was terribly impressed by him, more than can be said of anyone else he met. [S. W. S.]

never turned up. Whether it went to the bottom of the sea somewhere or is still gathering dust in some remote warehouse I never could find out.

Once in town I took Achi to a native restaurant, and we took tea together, raised eyebrows from passersby notwithstanding. My modest account with him was settled, and we sat and chattered about unimportant things that had nothing to do with our parting. Finally he stood rather suddenly and held out his hand. We shook quite solemnly, and Achi said simply, "Tabé, tuan." I never saw him or Nona again.

❧ 16 ❧

Back to Singapore and Portraiture for a
Living; Flying Snakes and Flying Foxes,
and Au Revoir to the Jungle

O NCE SETTLED IN MY HOTEL,
I procured a perfectly gorgeous 1929 Buick taxi and
drove to Pat Lawrence's house. This gentleman, on hearing strange footsteps entering his house, appeared in a
bright orange dressing gown and a thick coating of shaving soap. He was very surprised and pleased to see me
and promptly asked me to lunch.

The bright sun, crowded streets, flower- and tree-
bordered canals, hectically driven cars, and ultrafuturis-
tic buildings of Soerabaya very much reminded me of
Geneva. All along the main streets were a lot of new
buildings, mostly of variously colored stones or plaster-
covered brick, but all of the most violently modern style,
square-edged, flat-roofed, with weird, abrupt copings
and vast windows almost choked with massive stone bars

running both ways and projecting like a grating. These were filled with colored glass, which formed a cool twilight within (infinitely better for offices than the old open houses that admit all the heat, nay rather encourage it). We took lunch in a cool, quiet, small, excellently run, futuristically decorated club-restaurant in the basement of one of these buildings. It much resembled an airily decorated [Parisian?] "premier bar."

I spent the rest of the day wandering about the native shops and markets and found a beautiful ring to add to the collection I was making for my mother. Returning to my hotel, I found an invitation to dinner waiting for me from a family I had not met before but who knew Pat Lawrence, who had been so kind as to arrange it for me. They proved to be quite charming, and it was late before I got to bed. I left very strict instructions for the morning with the manager of the hotel, and a peremptory knocking roused me in time to eat some breakfast and repack before I had to leave.

Collecting all my belongings, I hired a taxi to take me to the boat. I noticed that my thirty-four traps had been placed religiously in the back of the luggage taxi, along with a fine assortment of empty tins and discarded bottles that I had been endeavoring to lose. Rage got the better of me at being thwarted in my ingeniously laid plan for unburdening myself, and I told the coolies that *"teda moe brancaps"** (don't want the blasted traps!) was the order of the day, whereupon a so far unwilling crowd

---

*In dictionary kitchen Malay this is *tida mau* . . . , though the last word puzzled even an Indonesian I asked; it may be *bungkus*, which means roughly "bundle." Spelling was not Ivan's strong suit. [S. W. S.]

of workers fell like ravening beasts upon these hated objects and divided them unfairly enough with surprisingly little argument. Lovingly they clutched cracked bottles of cyanide-impregnated cement, and boxes filled with dust and dead flies taken from a lamp globe. Consequently, the luggage taxi that followed us to the dock was totally obscured by white pants and brown legs. My boxes, including those picked up at the customs shed, were manfully borne to the deck of the ship by groaning little men holding feverishly to anything from one to ten muddy rat traps in their right hands.

There were a lot of people going by this boat to catch the mail steamer from Batavia [Djakarta] to Europe, as all the second-class cabins were filled with first-class passengers, and all these and their relations were on board when I arrived. I watched these departing and listened to their cries of *"Dar Dar!"* (roughly "good-bye") as we steamed out. A pilot took us out of the harbor and another took us right out to sea. I leaned over the bulwarks just as we were slowing down by a weird old hulk anchored miles out at sea, from which came a smart motor boat to take our pilot off. This took some time, and it rapidly became dark, and a most impressive sight arose. The sea was flat calm, the sky cloudless, and this old boat stood out black and grim against the flame-and-orange pastel hues of the setting sun, while stars shone brightly above and the night, black and hazy, closed us in on three sides. It was very still, not a breath of wind, not a sound of water; no wonder that a girl who had just left her people wept bitterly.

The next day when I awoke I found we were already lying in the roads off Semarang, surrounded by eleven other large boats. I got up and dressed leisurely, as I had no intention of going ashore. At midday regularly a certain wind blows up that is apt to prevent re-embarkation. However, I was much dismayed to find that breakfast was over and lunch laid at nine o'clock; but feeling none too well, I made no further agitation about food. I went back to sleep and did not wake again until six-thirty, when I found my cabin dark and deserted, my cabin companion's bed having been made and the room tidied while I slumbered. The companionship of a lovely American girl seemed to complete my cure, and though I didn't return to bed until quite late—or early, depending on one's point of view—I was up at 6:15 the next morning, dressed, and packed in time to watch our arrival at Tandjoengpriok, the port for Batavia.

A vast floating dock propelled by a tug alongside came up, and all the luggage and people for the mail boat were slowly deposited thereon. I waited till the last minute in order to give my card to my American friend, but could not find her and so gave it to her mother, while another passenger held up the tender for me. He was English and suffering from an awful skin rash, to get cured of which he was going to Singapore, so we had a long talk on boils and skin diseases.

On board the large gray mail boat I met a very polite and charming lot of pursers and stewards who arranged that I could sleep in the second class and eat, etc., in the first. None of the native cabin boys knew where No. 235 was, but after a bit I got all my heavy luggage into it and then immediately rushed ashore. I much surprised the taxi driver (who evidently thought me an American tourist) by telling him in Malay to go to a particular address "in double-quick time." Consequently we did. I thus said a final good-bye to those who had been most friendly on my first arrival in Java.

I should have liked to have spent more time in this exquisitely beautiful city. It had a wonderful air: the steam trams, the pretty natives, the old canals, the sunshine, the tropical gardens, long boulevards, and everything else.

I had breakfast with my friends, who then took me on the rounds to say good-bye to others I had met and to visit the native shops to buy some Birds of Paradise, as I could get them into England for them. However, the prices were prohibitive, so we had a final drink together and I returned to the boat.

I went to bed very late. Finding that all the portholes were closed, I opened everything up, and finally got to sleep. The next day passed as days on shipboard do, but I was glad to meet an Englishman who had been endeavoring for a long time to keep fish alive and had succeeded in getting some to the Soerabaya aquarium and intended sending some to the London Zoo.* We had a long talk about animals, and he gave me much to think about. I walked about by myself for a while and then retired to bed. The other fellow in the cabin refused to open the porthole, because he said the water would come in, although we were already among the islands [outside Singapore], would be anchored in an hour, and the porthole was about forty feet above the water!

My cabin mate's alarm clock woke me at six the next

---

*These presumably were tropical marine fish, but the general type, let alone species, is not specified in the diary. [S. W. S.]

morning as arranged, and I got up feeling more ghastly than I ever had before. By the time I had paid all my chits, I felt even worse, both mentally and physically, but managed to get to my hotel, where I collapsed, literally. A doctor was sent for, and I was told that I had an acute attack of nicotine poisoning resulting from indulging in a surfeit of Manila cheroots. It hurt like hell, and there was a Hindu band that thought it was playing jazz, that practiced all day in the enclosed courtyard.

Several days later, still bent double, I staggered out onto the verandah to get away from the alleged band and sat moping in a cane chair. I took along my sketchbook, since reading was impossible in view of the efforts of the musically inept gentlemen below. I tried sketching some of the animals I had last seen, and then I began doodling and drawing bits of the odd people who were passing in the street below. There happened to be a swarthy gentleman in a rumpled white suit and wearing thick horn-rimmed spectacles, slumped in a similar wicker chair on the verandah outside the room next-door to me. He watched me all afternoon and finally came over, asking very politely and in lilting tones to see my efforts. We became rather chummy, and I warmed to him when I learned he was a medical doctor and sympathetic to my pains. He then asked me if I did portraits, and I told him no, since a formal portrait was the last thing I felt like doing at that moment. He allowed as how this was a pity as he had always wanted his portrait painted, but with singular levity added that he supposed he was so stunningly ordinary to look at that nobody with artistic ability could whip up any enthusiasm for the chore.

Later that evening I got to thinking about this encounter and the fact that the good doctor had said he would drop in the next day to see how I was feeling. I had also been presented with my hotel bill to date, which had scared the daylights out of me. Being a European, I knew that as long as I was ill the management could not turn me out, for those were the days of the white man's burden and other such rubbish. However, these dicta worked both ways, so that a white man was not allowed to "lower" himself to the native level by "working" except in some approved white domain. In addition to an absence of money, I lacked any skill or even ability to gain employment in such exalted realms, so I was sort of at the end of my tether, considerably scared, as one usually is when ill and far from home, and faced with the necessity for doing something fast despite the aftermath of the cheroots and the very real contemporary competition of the alleged jazz band below. So I got hold of a large piece of paper and some pencils, propped myself up in bed, and contemplated my medical neighbor as an animal, and actually alive. It took my mind off things.

When the doctor arrived as promised the next day, I took a hard look at him and then rather tentatively showed him my effort. The result was most surprising. He at first showed every sign of amazement, then delight, but finally a kind of sneaky look came into his enormously expressive eyes. "Wonderful, wonderful!" he said, "But when did you take the photograph?"

I really felt like murdering the man, and I must have shown my emotion, for he literally yelped, and before I knew what he was up to, he had whipped out a checkbook and written out a positively enormous sum (for those days) in Straits dollars, which he offered me rather tentatively as if he expected me to bite him. When I accepted it, he started in on a long spiel about his eldest daughter who was getting married and just where she would hang his portrait. I was completely thunderstruck, paid my hotel bill, and got well very quickly. I had enough, in fact, for a ticket to Japan where funds were waiting for me if I could manage to get that far, and sufficient for another week in Singapore. I was determined to make a final foray into the jungle before I started my homeward journey through nontropical lands.

I was loth to go home at all, and bolstered by the doctor's check, I indulged in a series of daydreams in which I became quite incredibly famous for my monumental work in the East Indies, all financed, of course, by my portraits of the rich and noble. These fantasies, however, did not last very long, if only because I realized that among other things I should have to buy a complete new set of collecting equipment, having disposed of this before I sailed for Singapore. Too, I had had time to do some thinking while ill and had reached the painful conclusion that I must acquire proper zoological training if I was to do really valuable work in that field. Collecting specimens was all very well, but I had learned just enough to realize that this was not enough. Cambridge it would have to be—first.

I still had some letters of introduction for Singapore and now put these to use. All those I called on (well, almost all) were sympathetic, but they were also busy. As a last resort, since he was reputed to be a frightfully black sheep of the family, I called on an uncle, one of my father's brothers.* He proved to be delightful and promptly announced that he would arrange something somehow. He was working as a car salesman for one of the major import firms and either took or wangled several days off, because he turned up at my hotel one morning and barged in on me while I was still at breakfast. I am not at my best until *after* breakfast, but he was so keen to get started that I exerted myself and shortly thereafter we were headed north from Singapore into Johore at the tip of the Malay Peninsula.

From his comments it was clear that my uncle had never been in true jungle and had not the foggiest notion what it was like, despite having lived in Singapore for some years and having traveled fairly extensively through the islands, and I became a bit apprehensive as to where or into what he might take me. He proved, however, to have a brain as well as charm and had made enquiries among his friends.

The road at first was quite decent, and the car, judging by the smoothness of the ride, must have been provided with special springs of some kind, for even after we turned off the main road onto a narrow and hardly recognizable track, she still rode gently over the bumps. Even more a cause for wonder was the remarkably rational driving of the little Malay chauffeur, who showed no inclination to take hairpin bends on one wheel at sixty miles an hour or, indeed, to perform any of the other stunts that I had come to think of as obligatory for any

*Presumably he was a "black sheep" because he had sided with Ivan's mother when she and Ivan's father were divorced. [S. W. S.]

self-respecting driver in that part of the world. His driving lacked excitement but I was content, since I could look at the scenery instead of concentrating on hanging on. Later, when he was out of earshot, I asked my uncle about his extraordinary behavior and was informed with a grin that the little man had started out with normal lunatic habits but had been prevailed upon to reform. No details were forthcoming on how the transition had been accomplished, my uncle remarking simply that it had taken some time and considerable "persuasion"!

The road wound upward between neatly cultivated fields, with here and there a patch of forest or an open boggy meadow in which water buffalo grazed or lay at ease. These animals are common to all of Southeast Asia, and in many cases it is difficult to tell if a herd is "tame" or "wild." There may be a few herds of truly wild buffalo on a few of the islands, but most of the "wild" buffalo are feral animals,* and in some cases even these seem to belong to somebody and even to be used for work by their presumptive owners. They—including the domesticated ones—can be terribly dangerous, particularly to those who are strangers to them, but especially to "foreigners," though the native boys who care for them can beat them with virtual impunity. A number of Europeans, or white men generally, have been killed over the years when they have tried simply to take a photograph of one. So far as I know, no one has come up with a specific explanation for this, though it may have something to do with the smell of Europeans, which is quite

---

*"Tame" animals that have reverted to the wild state.

different from that of the native peoples. I always showed buffalo the greatest respect myself!

By midmorning we were well up in the mountains and soon turned off onto another track, much better than the one we had been on and showing signs of considerable and very recent labor. This wended its way between forest giants and led finally to a spacious and obviously new house set in the middle of an open area, manifestly just cleared of its entangling vegetation. The owner met us on the verandah and gave us a warm welcome, as did his very pretty wife who joined us a moment later. They had known my uncle in Singapore and were delighted to see him again, and made it clear that any nephew of his was a friend of theirs. We were promptly invited to stay to lunch, dinner, overnight, or whatever suited us, and my uncle accepted, telling them specifically why we were there. Our hosts expressed themselves as even more delighted, and it was agreed that after lunch I should lead an "expedition" into the surrounding forest.

During lunch they questioned me at length on my travels and on what the jungle was like, and we did not leave the table until rather late. The owner told me what he could of the area he had acquired for his plantation. It had been roughly surveyed, of course, and much of it was suitable for clearing and cultivation, but it was clear from what he said that there were patches of true primary jungle sprinkled about the place. By playing a variety of Twenty Questions with him, I managed to pin down what seemed to be the largest of these, which was also the closest to the house and ultimately proved to be the easiest to get into. I had no time to thoroughly investigate the geology of the place, but there must have been some sudden "break" of some kind, because this primary forest came virtually up to the lawn and then stopped, with almost no outer "wall" to be hacked through. There was a rather steep drop of nearly a hundred feet from the lawn, and then the forest began.

I warned my hosts that it was unlikely that we would see many animals in the short visit we planned, though monkeys and birds (and the ubiquitous insects) could probably be expected. They all looked politely disbelieving but said nothing, and for the moment I refrained from educating them further, though, in answer to a question, I did state that it was unnecessary to carry any heavy artillery with us, or even a revolver.

All of us having changed into suitable clothing—in their case, what they thought was suitable but which more resembled Hollywood's idea of jungle dress—we made our way to the edge of the "cliff." Here I went first, stamping out crude steps in the soft earth as best I could, but occasionally sliding for some distance, followed by my host, his wife, and then my uncle, the theory being that the two men would assist the lady. Truthfully, she was a much better climber than either to begin with, and since both were inclined to be portly, it really worked the other way, though she was far too tactful to even hint at such a thing.

And so we entered the jungle again. Perhaps it was the thought that I must soon leave this Eden to return to the cold and fogs of England and the confines of the classroom, but I wished suddenly that I were alone here. I remember muttering something to the effect that they should wait while I reconnoitered a bit, and they mur-

mured their agreement. I think they somehow under-
stood and respected my feelings, though nothing was
ever said. I did not go far, and what I thought in those
few minutes I cannot put into words, but I knew then that
I would come back, perhaps not to these jungles, but to
a jungle somewhere, somehow.

When I went back to the others, they were overhearty,
quite deliberately I think, probably sensing that I was still
feeling rather emotional about the whole business. However, the major point they made brought me quickly back
to current practical realities. They admitted freely that
they had thought I must be joking about animal life in the
jungle, having imagined it as a sort of zoo without bars
—tigers lurking behind every bush, snakes in every tree,
and a constant parade of smaller fry trotting past. Not
only were there no tigers, there were no bushes to speak
of, for this was true primary jungle, with little undergrowth. After a bit their chattering stopped, and I led
them further in, using a navigation system Achi and I had
worked out.*

We paused under a particularly magnificent jungle
giant, and I was once again bombarded with questions,
though now their voices were subdued, as if they felt it
would be sacrilege to shout. A troop of monkeys had
frolicked through the trees above us, and we could hear
the twittering of birds in the canopy, but otherwise had
seen no animals other than insects, and I was implored
to search out some animals for them. Now, this, of

---

*From a very few vague hints, this may have consisted of going left
around one tree and right around the next and so on, thus keeping them on a *more or less* straight line. I do not, however, guarantee this. [S. W. S.]

course, is easier said than done. In later years I had always to consult my diaries to convince myself of the falsity of my *own* impression that a particular jungle was surely far more full of life than the one I was in now. One tends to remember the highspots—catching or even just seeing animals—and to forget the sometimes prolonged periods during which *nothing* is seen and the days are filled with the dull routine of laying trap lines and inspecting them, filling out catalogues, dealing with the staff, etc., *ad nauseam.*

I attempted to explain to them the rhythm of the jungle. I had not at this time become truly aware of this as a rhythm, but I did know that certain times were much better than others for seeing animals. It was now about three o'clock, a period when all sensible animals were indulging in their afternoon siesta, but I knew from experience that in an hour or so they would start to move about, beginning their early-evening hunt for food, and our chances would improve. The others were more than willing to wait, so I used the time searching for a waterhole we could watch from a reasonable distance, but could find none. There seemed not to be any streams in our immediate area, though the ground was spongy everywhere (whether my host's superb London-made boots were ever the same again I don't know).

Returning to consult with our host, I explained the situation and asked if he knew of any watercourses on his plantation, since these would be the best places to watch for animals. He pondered a minute and then said that there was one, on the other side of the plantation, of course, at the bottom of a relatively shallow ravine. After some discussion, we agreed on a plan of action: to stay here for a time in the hopes that something might appear, and then to make an early-morning trek into the ravine the next day. The evening chorus began on schedule and "things" could be seen moving about in the canopy far above us, though as a "floor show" it was a complete failure, and we made our way back to the house, where we showered and dressed for dinner.

And I do mean "dressed." My uncle, appearing in a violently colored dressing gown as soon as he had showered, had poked his head into my room and hissed at me, "Evening dress, dear boy. They're very formal at dinner." I therefore hauled out my gentleman's "superb evening dress" and gave it a shake. Out fell a substantial collection of small paper packets, triangles, etc.: my collection from the Mentawis, which had somehow never been extracted from its temporary repository. I let out a yelp for a servant, who appeared on the run, and shortly had the suit properly brushed and fully presentable. In the meantime I gathered up my precious little packets and found a more suitable place to store them—no pun intended.

The gong rang, and we proceeded to the dining room, where our hostess was already waiting for us. I have said that she was pretty. With her hair more formally arranged and dressed for dinner in something diaphanous and flowing, she was really very beautiful. I suppose I must have gawped, for her husband promptly announced very solemnly that he was not going to risk going down the ravine *ahead* of me in the morning. This provoked a not unkind burst of laughter from the others, and from me, for she was at least twice my age and clearly devoted to her husband—but she was still beautiful!

However, my unspoken compliment pleased both of them, and dinner passed off with considerable hilarity as we traded stories, each trying to outdo the others.

We were just about to move onto the verandah for coffee and cigars—at this point I felt well enough to risk one of the latter—when a commotion was heard from just beyond the verandah. Our host went to see what the trouble was and soon returned carrying a much mangled snake, asking me what kind it was. It had been nearly chopped in four by the houseboys but, despite this, I could see that it was unusual, and with my host's permission I laid it out on the now cleared table to inspect it. To my delight—and chagrin, considering its condition—it proved to be a Flying Snake *(Chrysopelea)*. Of course, these do not fly or, apparently, even glide very far, despite some reports that leave one with a picture of the snake doing loop-the-loops between trees. But they can "flatten" themselves to some extent and, by straightening their bodies very rapidly, can launch themselves into space and land a fair distance away. There are several species, and I frankly did not know which this was, not having made snakes my specialty. Nor could I say with certainty whether it was poisonous or not, though I was fairly sure it was not really dangerous.

Several years later when I was working as a Demonstrator [roughly the equivalent of instructor in the United States] at Cambridge, a nonzoological junior professor suggested that I should be tossed out for talking rubbish: flying snakes, indeed! I disliked him anyway but should probably be grateful to him for providing a kind of "last straw." It was not long afterward that I left the formal academic world and returned to my beloved jungles.

My hosts, however, were keenly interested when I told them what little I knew about these snakes, and we talked long into the night. It was our hostess who finally pointed out that if we were to follow our plan for the morning, it might be a good idea to get some sleep first. And if I had any lingering notions of disposing of her husband, her motherly good-night kiss restored me to my proper status.

I was up at some truly ungodly hour the next morning and made a tour of the cleared area to see whether there might be a "better" jungle than we had visited the day before and/or to choose a route into the ravine my host had mentioned. I settled on the latter.

Thus it was that we breakfasted early and made our way down into the ravine, truly not a very deep one, choosing a convenient log on which to sit near the stream, which ran carelessly along a winding channel. At first all was silence except for the drip of water and an occasional twitter in the trees. And then some great bird called, and the jungle came to life.

We sat very still and waited as little rustling noises grew around and above us and the calls of birds and other animals burst forth. It was still early, but I was nevertheless very startled and delighted to see suddenly a diminutive deerlike form appear at the other side of the stream. This was a chevrotain, ordinarily nocturnal and a most retiring creature, apparently come for a last drink before seeking its hiding place for the day. Or perhaps it was in fact lost, since in Malaya they are ordinarily found in the lowlands. There are several species; that found in Malaya is called the Kanchil [a Malay word] Chevrotain (*Tragulus javanicus*) and has given rise to the saying "cunning as a kanchil." Apart from being (as a rule) hard to find in the first place, these little animals "play 'possum," feigning death until the hunter who thinks he's got one relaxes and rubs his hands in glee over his quarry—at which point the kanchil takes off, never to be seen again.

The Chevrotains, also called Mouse-Deer, are an exceedingly ancient stock and, though they look superficially like tiny deer, are anatomically more like pigs on the one hand and camels on the other. Their behavior is more akin to that of rodents than anything else. They measure about eighteen inches from nose to tail and are brown, with very distinctive white markings. The males have tiny tushes that are certainly more pig- than deer-like, and all mince about on tiny hooves.

We watched nearly breathless with excitement until it moved off—I had never seen one before—when three pairs of querying eyes asked me, "What was it?" In slow motion we went into a huddle, and I told them in a low voice what I knew it to be, and cautioned them not to whisper; whispers carry further and disturb animals more than ordinary but quiet speech.

Squirrels there were in plenty, and such as they had never seen before, even though they knew of more species than the ordinary Britisher or American has dreamed of. No dull gray or red and white these, but vivid oranges, yellows, golden browns, and blacks, with sometimes a bold pattern of stripes—I cannot remember which ones we saw that afternoon—darted about the

trees and squabbled on the ground before us. Monkeys
sailed overhead in flying troops, and birds could be
heard everywhere, though most could be seen only as
shadows or flashes of color flitting in the canopy. We
stayed in the ravine until late morning but saw only one
other "animal."

Just as we were about to leave, a spotted kitelike form
glided from one edge of the clearing to the other. It was
a kaguan, and I remembered The Place and my first
morning in The Jungle.

At lunch the others were plainly thoughtful, and it was
my uncle who spoke first, admitting that *all* his ideas
about the jungle had been knocked into the proverbial
cocked hat by our two brief visits there. Our hosts
agreed, and quizzed me once again on when and where
and how to look for animals. Some of my advice then was
undoubtedly very bad, since I had really very little experience and had been lucky, though I saw relatively few of
the animals that live in the jungles of the Oriental region.
I didn't even know of all of them, having spent my
"youth" compiling lists of African antelopes and Egyp-
tian dynasties! Nevertheless, I think I was of some help
to them; at least they never again thought of the true
jungle as something to be "hacked through, machete in
hand."

We left that afternoon and made our way sedately
down into the lowlands once again, hoping to reach Singapore before dark and in good time for a farewell dinner; my boat sailed the next morning. We turned onto
the main road as the sun sank low enough to emblazon
the clouds on the horizon, and my uncle leaned forward
and tapped the driver on the shoulder. He pulled over

and stopped immediately, and my uncle said rather formally, "Beautiful sunset, what?" It was. I just nodded, and we sat there for some time watching as the clouds drifted like some fluid kaleidoscope, ever shifting in shape and color. And then our little Malay said, "*Kalong,*" and pointed to the east.

Fox-Bats (*Pteropus,* etc.), or so-called Flying Foxes,* were flying with measured wing strokes in great streamers across the sky to visit their evening feeding grounds. Some of these bats have bodies the size of ravens and a wingspread that measures over five feet. Their faces are foxlike and lack any odd appendages, and even their ears are simple pricked ears. They come in all sorts of colors —there are a number of species, and they are found all over the Orient from northern Australia almost to Japan and also in Madagascar and other islands off Africa, though not in that continent itself—and some are relatively small, but all have the same general appearance, and they can do an enormous amount of damage, especially to citrus crops. Most live in colonies, and each night at sundown they fly forth in vast cohorts from their daytime resting places, traveling in long lines or streamers, not darting as do most other bats, but proceeding in orderly fashion almost like massed flights of airplanes. Though they are a rowdy, irascible bunch when roosting or feeding, they are one of the most impressive sights in the clear evening skies of an Oriental sunset. I had seen

---

*Some are on exhibit at the Philadelphia Zoo (in what a friend of mine calls the "red-light district"), and I will never forget overhearing an obvious nonzoologist remark to his family, "Flying-Foxes. I dunno; they look like bats to me." [S. W. S.]

252 /

them many times before. It was long after dark when we reached Singapore.

My uncle and I stopped at my hotel, where I had my bags taken back to my room, and then went on to a private club-restaurant where we had a very quiet dinner together, talking long into the night. I was charged with various messages to my mother, and we tacitly agreed that should he come to London, he would be our guest. It was nearly three when we returned to my hotel. My uncle declined to come in and wished me *bon voyage* on the steps. The next morning I sailed for Hong Kong and home.

A Recipe for Nasi Goreng

Technically, Ivan's recipe was not *nasi goreng,* which means fried rice—we boiled ours—but the name seems to refer generally to any dish containing rice and whatever else you may wish to put in it. The recipe that follows is open to experimentation, and Ivan sometimes added other meats (veal in particular), but this may be looked on as fairly basic.

The recipe given here will feed about ten people for one meal or, as in Ivan's case, one person for about ten nights: it will keep that long provided—and this is very important—you reheat it *thoroughly* every night. It must also be pointed out that not everyone will be able to eat it; if your stomach rebels at spicy foods (as mine does), don't try it. The amount of spice you use is up to you, but to cook it without spices is pointless.

Boil one package (one pound) of rice according to the directions on the package, but do not add any shortening (and don't use "instant" rice). Be sure it is properly salted.

The next two ingredients you may have to get at a Chinese grocery, or they may be available in gourmet food shops: dried black mushrooms (do not use the little button mushrooms generally available) and dried shrimp. Fresh shrimp can be substituted for these latter, but if you use fresh shrimp, add them at the end. The dried mushrooms and shrimp should be set to boil in separate pots. Don't use too many of either; they expand, you know! Once these have boiled, pour off the water, cover with fresh water, and boil again; repeat, and allow to boil until both are nice and tender. Go by appearance and feel. Once cooked, chop up the mushrooms (not too small) and remove any hard or woody pieces. Leave the shrimp whole; they'll fall apart eventually anyway.

While these are boiling, put some vegetable oil in an iron skillet and dump in sliced onions and coarsely chopped green peppers. You'll have to experiment on amounts here. I would suggest two good-sized peppers, and don't skimp on the onions. Cook until soft, and then add a coarsely chopped medium cabbage (cut out the hard core—you can nibble on this while cooking). Once the cabbage has softened, add ground red pepper and dark brown chili powder. If you have the right kind of stomach, you can check on how much you want by taste. I went by the aroma and the fact that my nose tickled properly when I had added sufficient for Ivan's palate. Stir and continue cooking until the vegetables are done but not, heaven forbid, soggy.

When the rice is done, dump it into a large pot. If you have an enormous double boiler, fine; otherwise, choose a pot with rigid handles so that you can put this in an even larger pot with water in the bottom, thus producing a makeshift double boiler. Add curry powder to the rice, again to taste or smell, etc., and stir well. Also, if you can get it (and you can bear it), add some sambal. This is occasionally available in gourmet food departments. There may be other brands or types, but I used Conimex Sambal Boedak, and Ivan liked a bottle and a half in his *nasi goreng*. You may not want so much; just sniffing a bottle that had been opened for two years made my nose twitch. Now dump in the shrimps, mushrooms, vegetables, or whatever else you are trying; stir thoroughly to mix it all up, and continue heating in the double-boiler arrangement. About half an hour is all right, though if you do serve it on successive nights, you will find that it improves daily. But, again, be sure to heat it thoroughly every day.

Serve with a soft fried egg on top, and/or with fried bananas. And if it blows the back of your head off, remember that I've warned you.

Index

Index

British Museum, 37
Bromo hotel, 116
Bromo volcanic cone, 118–120
bubonic plague, 22
Buddha, 19, 115
Buddhism, 19
buffalo, 242–243
Burak, Malay States, 26
Burke, Billie, 48
Burroughs, Edgar Rice, 8

C

Cambridge (university), 5–6
Caribbean Treasure (Sanderson),
　xiv
cassowary, 178, 199–200
cats, 219, 219n
Ceylon, 13–20
chevrotains, *see* Mouse-Deer
Chinese, attitude toward Malays,
　29; Malay opinion of, 28
civets, 56–57, 212
closed-canopy forests, 8–9
Clouded　Leopard　(*Profelis
　nebulosa*), 219
Cobego, *see* Kaguan
Colombo, Ceylon, 13–14
Colugo, *see* Kaguan
Corbett, Jim, 66, 68
Crab-eating Macaques (*Cynamol-
　gus irus*), 123–124
crabs, 100
crocodiles, 101
crows, 101
Cuscus (*Phalanger*), 191–194

D

Denpasar, Bali, 125
Dermaptera, 39

djanghael, 7–10
Djokja (Djakarta), Java, 112–114
Dodinga, Ternate, 172
Draco volans, 94
durians, 143

E

eagle, 101
Edinburgh, Scotland, 4
Eels, North American Congo
　(*Amphiuma means*), 37
equatorial forests, 8–9;
　bio-temporal rhythms in, 45–
　47;
　in Ceylon, 22–23;
　developmental stages, 50–52;
　light in, 47;
　in Malay States, 32–53, 244–
　246, 249–252;
　in Maykor Island, 188–189;
　in Sumatra, 84–96, 216–218;
　upper canopy, 86–87
Eton, 6

F

fauna division, *see* Wallace's Line
feral animals, 242n
Fiddler Crabs (*Uca*), 100
Fish Eagle (*Haliaetus leucogaster*),
　101
"floating" pebbles, 126–127
Flying Foxes (*Pteropus*), 252
flying lizards (*Draco*), 93–94
Flying Snakes (*Chrysopelea*), 248
forests, *see* equatorial forests,
　sacred forest (Bali), and tropi-
　cal forests
Fox-Bats, *see* Flying Foxes
frogs, 99

Index